Back to the Pulpit

Best wishes,

Jack.

John Richardson.

By the same author:

Jack in the Pulpit
Jack in the Navy
Jack in the Spirit

Back to the Pulpit

More memories of a country parson

Jack Richardson

Illustrated by Henry Brewis

Bridge Studios
Northumberland
1990

First published in Great Britain in 1990

by Bridge Studios,
 Kirklands,
 The Old Vicarage,
 Scremerston,
 Berwick upon Tweed,
 Northumberland TD15 2RB.

 Tel: 0289 302658/330274

ISBN 1 872010 45 8

Typeset by EMS Phototypesetting, Hide Hill, Berwick upon Tweed.

Printed by Martin's of Berwick Ltd.

Foreword

'Jack; you're an amazing man! I have climbed the Jungfrau, skied in Finland, tramped in America and camped in the Hebrides and everything went as planned. Nothing extraordinary ever happened. In a way it was all dull because things always worked out as we had meant them to do. But you can just cross the road and something will happen to you that is almost beyond imagination,' said the Vice-principal of my theological college.

I suppose he was right. There are people like me to whom things seem to happen in an extraordinary yet natural way. Sometimes I have tried to make things happen and it just hasn't worked out.

For instance, I was a regular fan at Newcastle United Football Club. The man who sat in front of me in the stand was a high-up official of the Boiler-makers' Union. He used to swear like a trooper! The air would turn blue and he always turned round to seek confirmation from me that the referee was illegitimate, blind and sub-normal mentally.

So I decided to wear my clerical collar to a match and have the delight of seeing his expression when he realized I was a clergyman.

What happened? Nothing; and why?

'Where's Jim today?' I asked when I noticed his empty seat.

'Didn't you read in the papers that he died. He was buried last Saturday. United were playing away!'

Then there are times when I could expect something to happen and it didn't.

'Vicar, I must warn you that my step-father is dangerous. He is violent and could get nasty with you if you say anything he does not like!'

So said the stepson to me at his mother's funeral.

'There is a possibility that a manslaughter charge could be brought against him. He battered my mother so much that she has died from injuries and the police are making enquiries. Please be careful about what you say for he'll up and bash you at the slightest provocation.'

So I was prepared for something to happen. He followed the coffin into the crematorium chapel. He looked an aggressive, ignorant bully. In fact he rather looked like a battling gorilla!

'Don't worry,' said Norman the superintendent, 'I'll have two of my men at the back of the chapel and at the faintest hint of trouble they'll fettle him.'

Nothing happened; in fact he congratulated me on the service! He didn't congratulate the judge who separated him from society for four years!

I have written in one chapter that the main ingredients are truth; humour and a little embroidery! I can assure the reader that all the stories are fundamentally true. Told by themselves they could be dull but with a sparkle of fun and a descriptive embroidery they are transformed yet remain non-fiction.

I do hope that you will enjoy reading this book as much as I have enjoyed writing it.

Jack. (John Richardson).

Hatches

The grave-digger kicked the clinging clay from his hob-nailed boots, wiped his bare forearm across his mouth and gazed down with pride at the six feet by three feet excavation he had just completed. A camouflage of artificial grass lay beside the resultant heap of earth. He wished to share his accomplishment with me.

'Hey, Jack,' he greeted me, 'that's a beauty, isn't it,' he remarked enthusiastically, and even lovingly, referring to the newly dug narrow bed awaiting its permanent tenant, 'You'll never get a better one than that.'

He looked at me as if he was sizing me up for future activities. I shuddered. Like undertakers one never knows what is behind the conversation of gravediggers. I once fell into a grave and the grave-digger waiting to fill it in seemed upset when they hauled me out of it. In Harry's case, however, he did not want me as a client for the execution of his no doubt skilful and exact six foot explorations but for a totally different, and indeed living, service. Somehow one does not readily associate grave-diggers with small, healthy, bouncing bairns. They seem, rather, to haunt cemeteries like ghouls spawning corpses and coffins.

'Will you do me a favour, Jack?' he asked me as he tossed his spade into a wheelbarrow and sat on a nearby convenient gravestone. I was more than troubled. I had no desire to keep him in further employment and his sweat-grimed T-shirt bore the logo, 'It could be your turn' and depicted an empty beer glass. As I looked at the shirt the motto became personal and the beer glass an hour glass. Shivering, I replied cautiously, 'Of course I will, if I can.'

'You alright, Jack?' Harry asked.

'Yes; someone just walked over my grave,' I replied,

averting my gaze from the opened earth towards a pair of mating collar doves. 'What do you want of me?'

'A baptism!'

'Hum! I always thought that you were a heathen,' I teased, 'but you'll be too heavy for me to take you in my arms. Fancy you wishing to be baptised. Are you not feeling too well?'

'No; not me. It's the babby. I had one six months ago.'

I knew that grave-diggers were a separate breed and of the prophecy that man born of man will live forever and I guessed that Harry's baby must have been born with a spade in its hand.

'Congratulations! I must ask if it is wise for you to be doing such strenuous, manual labour so soon after your labour. Who's the father?' I asked, fearful that it could be the sculptor for he had peopled the cemetery with an angelic host.

'Come off it Jack. You know what I mean. Can you baptise our bairn in a month's time?' he asked as he offered me a bribe; a mint with a hole, specially minted of course for grave-diggers.

'I'm willing to do this for you, Harry, but you must obtain the permission of your own parish priest. Have a word with your vicar after you've been to church next Sunday.'

Harry's spade almost jumped from the wheelbarrow as he laughed in derision.

'Church on Sunday! You're kidding. I get enough of church here in this cemetery; "Ashes to ashes, dust to dust...if God won't have you the devil must". I've heard it all but I'll go to see him tonight,' promised the sexton with one more appraising look at his latest accomplishment.

So the preparations for a baptism were begun in those grim surroundings. No wonder it turned out to be a most extraordinary christening.

I was at the church early. The vicar had kindly completed the baptismal register for me. I noted that the baby's name was to be Nathaniel.

The church door opened. In came the whole cemetery staff; superintendent, clerk, grave-diggers, and grass-cutters. They looked around at their strange surroundings and as there were no spades around on which to lean they asked me, 'Where do we sit?'

'Nowhere; you stand; over there,' I indicated.

They arranged themselves in pious position ranked six feet by three.

'No; that won't do. Looks like a funeral. Stand over there and leave room for the family.'

They repositioned and looked uncomfortable. The wailing of a child indicated the approach of the baptismal party. Strangely the infant was carried, not by a godmother but by the godfather. He was about five feet tall and equally as wide and would have made a good godfather for the Mafia.

'Would you like to give the baby to a godmother?' I suggested. In a strong stentorian, Glaswegian declaration of intent he simply indicated a negative answer.

The service progressed until I needed to take the child into my arms.

'Name this child.'

'Matthew!'

Quietly I whispered to the Scot, 'It's Nathaniel.'

'No way; Matthew.'

Daring to risk his Celtic ire I repeated tremulously, 'It's Nathaniel.'

'Aa sed Matthew and aa ken ma rights,' the godfather asserted.

'Your rights?' I queried.

'Aye. It's the godparents wha' gi' the bairn its name,' he insisted.

'Very well, I'll ask the godmothers and we'll have a concensus of opinion.' It was a wasted endeavour for they were his sisters. They shrugged their pretty Caledonian shoulders and giggled.

'Matthew!'; the church timbers rattled like bones. I turned to the parents.

'Matthew?'

'Nathaniel!'

'Matthew!!' exploded the pocket-sized Caledonian god-father. I tried to resolve this deadlock and asked the parents in desperation, 'What's wrong with Matthew?'

'He'll get Matt when he grows up.'

I persisted, 'What'll he get if he's called Nathaniel?'

Both factions were deeply entrenched. The godmothers giggled; the cemetery staff muttered lowly about 'bait-time' and the baby decided that time was not on its side and proceeded to wash my surplice.

'What I will do,' I informed them, 'is to baptise the baby Nathaniel Matthew.'

'NO!!' the warring Scot called, his sporran bristling like an outraged ridge-backed haggis, 'Matthew Nathaniel.'

I decided that I was the boss;
'Nathaniel Matthew, I baptise you.'
Poor bairn; Nat Mat!
'Will you come to our house for tea?' Harry invited me,
but with visions of grabbing, guzzling grave-diggers devastating any tea table, I refused. I was also fearful lest the
caber-tossing Glaswegian might express his disapproval to
me in physical terms. 'O.K. then,' said Harry, 'when you're
down for a funeral I'll bring you a piece of cake.'
Two days later I had to officiate at a funeral in that
crematorium. As I walked up the cemetery drive with the
undertaker in his claw hammer suit my intoned sentences;
'We brought nothing into this world etc,' were rendered
meaningless by Harry's loud interjection;
'I've brought you some cake.'
'And it is certain we cannot carry anything out,' I
concluded only to be negated by the insistent Harry who
declared,
'It's in the bait cabin; you can take it with you.'
I could scarcely curb my impatience. No sooner was the
service over than Harry escorted me to the small canteen
room set aside for weary grave-diggers to rest their bones
and eat.
'Jack, you'll never guess what happened,' remarked
Harry.
I was afraid to guess.
'When we got home after the baptism and removed the
tea towel which had covered the baptismal cake we found
that my brother had scraped the name Nathaniel from the
cake, had melted down three Mars bars and with them had
written Matthew on the cake.'
My mind boggled. As we entered the bait cabin, my
stomach turned. On one end of a wooden form stood an ex-
army haversack. Protruding from a top corner was the
piece of cake. A mouse had chewed the foil in which the
cake was wrapped and it hung there inflated with currants
and spice and all things nice! Harry knocked the opportunist rodent from its fruitful perch. With his pocket knife,

used mainly for scraping excess clay from his boots, he cut away the portion of cake which had been contaminated by the wee creature.

'That will be alright now,' he promised. 'Enjoy it!'

Matches

'Ecumenical' is a word that does not easily run off the tongue. Loosely translated it refers to world-wide Christianity. I'm all for it. I'll preach anywhere to any congregation; non-Conformist; the Church of Rome; the Church of Turkey or to non-Cangoists.

So with an ecumenical urge pounding through my veins and the promise of Scottish hospitality I journeyed to the Trossachs. I was to make sure that at least one Caledonian couple were correctly joined in Holy matrimony albeit in a Church of Scotland; to Sassenachs, the Presbyterian Kirk; and by an Anglican priest.

The parish had a lady minister with a good Biblical Christian name, Ruth, and a surname reminiscent of difficult days; Mendicant. Shades of gleaning in the cornfields! This particular marriage hastened her resolve to retire early. She now lives in pastoral peace and tranquillity among the kylies and mountain goats endeavouring to obliterate the memory of that fateful decision to allow Jack to conduct that wedding.

The bride lived a full twenty-five yards from the kirk door. A gleaming white Rolls Royce stood outside her parents' home ready to convey her. With white shutters newly painted and clean curtains up at the windows the house betrayed the opulence of the occupier. The bride's golden tresses fringed her head with a glorious halo and from that down to her golden shoes, she was a heavenly vision; like the sirens which lured sailors to their doom! I called in on my way to the church. Already there was a glint of victory in the bride's eyes. Her mother's eyes reflected deep relief. Her father expressed reluctance 'te gae her awa' but that emotion was tempered by the hope of his future financial improvement.

'I know I'm early, but I want to see the geography of the church and at the same time warn the groom of the dangerous waters ahead,' I said to all and sundry; aunts, uncles, cousins and hangers-on who, like the astrologers of the East came bearing gifts although there was little gold and no frankincense or myrrh. Among the multitude of table lamps, mirrors, pyrex dishes and glass vases I saw a useful present; a cookery book from the groom's mother. There was a large rolling pin but the attached instruction suggested that it should be employed belabouring the groom rather than bashing pastry.

The vestry door swung heavily on its hinges. In walked Bonnie Prince Johnnie and his best man. They were a brave sight for any man-hungry Scots lassie. Both were in full Highland dress; white frills neatly goffed, leather covered buttons, yards of tartan kilts and distinctive sporrans.

'Och aye, the noo,' I greeted them in the vernacular.

John smiled wanly; his best man replied, 'Is this the right place?'

Fearing that he could not distinguish a kirk from a but and ben I assured him 'Aye it is.' I was enjoying my Scots vocabulary. John sighed deeply. His manly figure drooped as was expedient for one about to surrender his independence and freedom. He looked desperately around for some avenue of escape. Ken's sporran seemed to be bulky.

'What hae'ye in ya' sporran?' I enquired. 'Was the deer pregnant when it was shot?'

The lady minister began to sag.

'Och, no,' replied Ken, 'it's a bag o' rice!'

'John, would you please sit here and check the details in the register?' I requested.

John sat; he perused, he bent double and remained stuck

fast. Motherly minister Ruth hastened to him, 'You alright? John.' His only answer was a soulful groan. He had cramp of the stomach. The muscles were as tight as wire stays. Ken and I endeavoured to prize him upright to no avail. John's groans drowned the invading chords of the organ voluntary. Desperately we tried everything from gentle persuasion to violent jerks. We couldn't allow him to meet his bride looking like Quasimodo!

'Stop it!' cried the alarmed minister, 'You'll tear his muscles. Get by; let me try.' She stroked his hair and whispered sweet nothings into his ear together with suitable biblical texts. The latter performed the miracle. 'Is there a lavatory here?' asked the anxious groom urgently. He came out of it after having been terribly sick.

'Sit down again, John,' said the ministering angel who resumed the soothing massage again and eventually John began to relax. To relieve the tension and to break the awkward silence now that no groans rent the air and the organist must have been sorting out his music, I spoke to Ken.

'By the way, is there one ring or two?'

'Only the one,' replied the best man.

'Well, have it ready and don't put it on your own finger for safe keeping. I once had a best man who put the ring on his little finger. The church was very warm. The finger swelled up and at the required moment he couldn't remove the ring.'

'No fear of that,' answered Ken, 'I'm not that daft. In any case it's too small to fit any of my fingers.'

He groped within his sporran. He went pale. He desperately explored the hidden recesses of his sporran. The muscles on his face had spasms. Finally he withdrew the bag of rice and emptied the contents over the register. He gave another look into the vacancy of his sporran and then stuttered, 'I've left it at home!'

There was a deathly hush. John's stomach reacted; Ruth began reciting passages from the Bible; me from the Koran until Ruth declared, 'Well, you'd better go and get it.'

'Do you live nearby?' I asked.

'No; about six miles up the glen; but dinna fash yersells, I'll be back in a flash.'

'Be careful how you drive!' cautioned the solicitous minister.

'Drive? I canna drive!' and Ken disappeared.

He dashed across the road and commandeered the Rolls and its driver. I went into the body of the church. The bride's mother, bless her, had lost her composure and sense of relief and had by now chewed her finger nails down to the quick. I told the gathered faithful that all was well but that there was time to dash out for a haggis baff and a pint. In the bride's house Devinia did a flop and her dad had a nervous spasm as they saw the Rolls and Ken leave them stranded so far from the altar.

The November day had darkened with the threat of snow as the bride and groom eventually left the church as man and wife. Then began a twenty mile marathon over and through the hairpin bends and forest firs of the Trossachs to the outback where the reception was to be held.

'I'm not looking forward to the journey,' I remarked to the minister, 'I don't know the road and don't relish driving in this gloom.'

'Then leave your car here,' she suggested, 'and I'll take you.' The minister, once behind the wheel became the monster. The Reverend Jekyll became Mrs Hyde. With her fangs bared and her bible on the back seat she overtook everything and everyone as the tyres screeched their protest around the bends. We arrived before the bride!

In the hotel foyer waitresses bearing liquid refreshment lined either side; on the left the whisky wenches and on the right the lemonade lasses.

'Phew,' said Ethel after our supersonic dash, 'lead me to a whisky!'

'Better stick to soft drinks,' I counselled, 'We've got the minister with us and she probably frowns on the hard stuff.'

Ethel picked up a large glass of diluted orange juice. The minister made a bee-line for the whisky.

'I've a wee cold,' she said as she gurgled down the first dram in one gulp and immediately picked up a second. We went into the lounge. The minister took a third measure of her medicine from a perambulating waitress then sank back into her chair and went fast asleep.

We had finished the main course of the meal when the head waiter placed a gavil beside my plate.

'What's this for?' I demanded.

'You're to propose the health of the bride and groom,' the resplendent boss told me.

'No; no; you've got it wrong. It's the bride's father who does that.'

'Not in Scotland, sir; it's the minister.'

'Oh well, that's O.K.; give it to Ruth,' I instructed with relief. Ruth laughed.

'I'll no be here for the speeches. I've got to get to Dunkeld to meet a train.'

'But you're my chauffeur. How will I get back? Walk?' I protested.

'Och; someone will take you. You'll not be stranded.'

I stood to speak. An expectant hush fell upon this gathering of highland outlaws and cut-throats as they directed their gaze through the malt mist towards me.

Before I could speak I saw the most ridiculous hat that I have ever seen. Description beggars me. I burst out laughing. Others began to laugh without knowing why I was laughing and so I laughed all the more. Tears ran down my cheeks. My stomach ached. It was what I would term as a good belly laugh. As I gained control, Margaret, the young aunt of the bride groaned as her laughter hurt and with a sharp intake of audible breath she began again laughing so heartily that it had a chain effect. This prompted a resumption of my laughing and now all the guests were doubled up with merriment and no speech was either required, necessary or possible. It was a great success.

Away from the claymores, the drams and the glens and in the more civilised uplands of Northumberland, the cradle of English Christianity, I made history by marrying a couple in a home – the very first such ceremony after the law was passed enabling this.

'I now pronounce you man and wife.'

The groom was too infirm to rise to kiss his bride. He was eight-seven years old and she was a stripling of eighty-four. The staff positioned their wheelchairs so as their lips could seal the union. The congregation was other members of this old peoples' home and no doubt I could recognise the gleam of hope in the age-worn faces of many of them. I expected the flood gates of matrimony to sweep like a flood through the establishment.

Three months afterwards I saw the bride and groom sitting in the dayroom. They were holding hands and had a certain serenity about them. She was wearing her wedding frock and carpet slippers.

'I'm disappointed in you both. You've been married now for three months and still there's no baby on the way!' I teased.

She took me seriously.

'It's not his fault, vicar; it's mine. I'm past it now.'
Bless her.

'Jack, will you officiate at a wedding for me?' said Alan, a vicar of a town parish, 'I've got to be away for a week.'

I arrived at his church early to ascertain the layout of the place. I did not know anything about the bridal couple and was looking for the vestry and the registers when an elderly gentleman came into the church. He was stooped but not enough to hide his black eye. It was a beautiful shade of purple and black.

'Where do you want me to sit?' he enquired.

'Are you a friend of the bride or groom?' I asked.

'I am the groom!'

'Oh, and what have you done to your face?' I asked.

'Walked into the edge of a door; couldn't see it,' was the quiet reply.

'How old are you?'

'Eighty-three,' whispered the groom, 'and my bride is

seventy-six.'

'Come with me and we'll check the registers in the vestry.' He took my arm and I helped him to avoid doors and stone pillars. On looking at the register I noted that his name was Abraham and that his bride Mary's age was given as eighty-three also.

'Mary's eighty-three,' I said, 'not seventy-six as you told me.'

'That's right; but she doesn't like anyone to know. It's to be a quiet wedding,' Methuselah remarked, 'we don't want any fuss.'

The church was crowded. The Over-Sixty Club had joined forces with the Railway Veterans' Association and many of the public were there because they had seen the television cameras outside the church. I met the bride in the porch.

'Will you give my grand-daughters time to lift me up after I've been kneeling. I've got arthritis in both knees,' she requested.

'That's alright, Mary,' I said, 'You need not kneel.'

'What?'

I raised my voice. 'You need not kneel!'

'What do you say?'

'You need not...never mind,' then to the bridesmaids, 'Follow me.' She knelt. I yelled. The grand-daughters did their heaving.

In my address I lightheartedly referred to Abraham's wife, Sarah, who conceived when she was allegedly eighty years old.

'There are baptisms here on Sundays,' I teased not knowing that numbers of the Press were occupying the back pews. What a press I received but there was worse. The television wanted a shot of me with the bridal couple. The groom had to be supported as the ceremony had taxed his strength. I hid his two sticks.

'Give them some advice, Jack,' called out one of the TV crew. I complied.

'Black his other eye and let him know who's the boss,' I

said to the bride who nodded her head and said, 'Nowhere; we're just staying at home.'

The following day my Rural Dean came to lunch.

'Can I watch the last few overs of the morning's play at Lords?' asked the cricket fanatic.

So while we sipped coffee and watched England's feeble efforts at bowling and with non-ecclesiastical comments from the Rural Dean, stumps were drawn and the Northern mid-day news came on the television.

'Hello; that's you,' said the Dean as the previous day's wedding flashed on the screen. The commentator did the talking. My lips were seen to move but thankfully my advice to the new bride was not given.

'What were you saying to them, Jack? Some words of wisdom, no doubt?'

Dispatches

'Clear lower deck! Hands muster on the sweep deck.'

The shrill pitch of the bosun's pipe alerted us. All ready in cassock, surplice, hood and scarf I awaited my summons to go aft to the minesweeping deck.

The First Lieutenant came into the wardroom; 'Ready when you are, padre.'

The captain, ship's company and about half a dozen mourners were grouped about the minesweeping gear. All engines and machinery were stopped. The ship presented herself broadside to the sea. The silence was terrific. Gone was the ubiquitous drone of the air-conditioning. The deck did not throb to the tune of the engines and the turn of the screw. Only the breeze in the rigging hummed its requiem and an occasional seagull squawked its final tribute. It is well known that seagulls are the departed souls of mariners!

The coffin lay on the slide which declined towards the swelling sea which was to be the tomb of our shipmate until the seas give up their dead. This sea seemed to be reluctant to receive him.

'We therefore commit his body to the deep.'

The wind sighed; the mourners wept; the joiner withdrew the bolt and the coffin began its grim journey which turned out to be a return trip.

As the coffin slid downwards an extraordinary large swell reared up crashing its volume and force against our ship. The waters covered us. The coffin came back inboard to rest grotesquely in an unseamanlike fashion athwart the sweep gear. I was more unfortunate than the sodden ship's company. I was thrown against a winch and knocked unconscious. The captain almost made it over the side!

I awoke.

20

I thought that, probably by mischance, I had been transported into Heaven for when I opened my eyes I saw a ministering angel who was pouring a heavenly nectar into my mouth. The brandy gave my ecclesiastical robes a spirit dimension. The angel was the First Lieutenant.

'Good God!' he exclaimed on seeing me open my eyes and then he took a generous gulp of the medicine himself. Of course he was mistaken; I was the padre; God's agent, not the Deity Himself!

I sustained three severely bruised ribs and had to be landed and taken to the nearest hospital for X-ray. I was strapped up and allowed to rejoin the ship. In the confusion no one had remembered to hoist the white ensign from its half-mast position until a keen signalman on an outgoing frigate in the Firth of Forth with a queer sense of humour asked 'Is the ship's cat dead?' to which our captain replied, 'Thanks; curiosity killed it!'

'What happened to the coffin?' I asked.

'Oh; the Jonty and the engineer officer heaved it overboard,' I was informed, 'and the Jonty had given the final committal "Go over and stay over!" And who dare to disobey the Master-at-arms?'

It was not a vindictive sea that caused my next calamity. The wind played tricks; it held its breath; it puffed and huffed then gusted with momentary gale force. The old yew tree in the churchyard groaned and creaked like a rheumatic limb while the wind-tossed floral tributes from other graves were blown to the boundary wall.

'This wind will dry up the earth after all the rain we've had,' remarked old Joe who had put a black tie around his collarless neck. His crumpled off-white shirt was partly obscured by a black and white scarf and his heavy brown boots kept him firmly anchored to the ground. He had been the dead man's 'marra'. He had also inherited old Billy's racing pigeons. I stood at the head of the grave as the undertaker supervised the lowering of the coffin. There was a great deal of water lying in the bottom of the grave and the sexton had tried to disguise this by emptying a barrow load of grass cuttings into it. Despite this only the coffin lid was discernible above the flood. I looked down and hoped that old Bill had a waterproof shroud otherwise he might catch his death of cold. I almost caught mine!

'Ashes to ashes; dust to dust; we brought nothing into...hang on there; give a hand,' I shouted desperately as the wind gusted to a devastating force ten catching my surplice and filling it out like a parachute. I was blown forward. The waterlogged ground beneath my feet crumbled. I tried to gain a foothold by digging my feet more firmly but all in vain. I joined our late, lamented brother Bill in his narrow and permanent bed hoping that it was not to be permanent for me. Bill was lying recumbent while I stood, six feet down, vertical. I prayed that the

coffin lid was not made of plaster board. Bill would have died of shock if I had crashed in! Johnny the undertaker reached down to me and heaved me back to sea level. My surplice was heavy with wetness and clay and my hands were grimey but I still held the prayer book and took up my stance to resume.

'There was no need for you to stamp on him: it's not in the book, you know. When we put them down they stay down,' rebuked Johnny.

> There was a lad was born in Kyle,
> but what na day o' what na style
> I doubt it's hardly worth the while
> to be sae nice to Robin.

So Robbie Burns of Ayrshire and immortal memory wrote on looking back upon his own birth in 1759. Thoughts of him conjure up for us pleasing vistas of Argyll; the Clyde; Bonnie Scotland and 'a man's a man for a' that'. He ennobled the humble haggis and aroused the sweetness of sorrowful parting with his,

> and we'll tak' a cup o' kindness yet
> for auld lang syne.

Despite the broad wealth of his writings Robbie never wrote a word about crematoriums. I canna' see the Scots wasting anything! The nearest he ever got to the subject was in 'Tam o' Shanter', when he wrote something like this;

> Tam; Tam; ye'll get ya' fairin'
> Hell will roast ya like a herrin';
> Like a herrin' or like a troot
> once ye're in ye'll never get oot!

How true of a crematorium and of the non-local establishment to which I had to journey to officiate at the funeral service of an old matelot. A garage opposite the gates had a huge sign which read, BODY SHOP. When I pointed this out to the proprietor he had faced me in the direction of the cemetery gates and pointed out the traffic sign, ONE WAY ONLY.

The furnace operator was called Robbie Burns although at his working-men's club he was known as Cinders. He always donned a clean, white shirt on the first day of every month, changing it only when the old month died. By then it was a dusty, charcoal colour. In warm weather he was known to wear his shirt for two months as he more than often worked stripped to the waist; bare bust! One could not then ascertain if his upper body was ashen as he was covered with tattoos. A huge, bald eagle clawed up his spine with its outstretched wings tucking themselves into the sweaty recesses of his armpits while its talons reached to his nether regions. His chest was hallowed ground in that it bore the words of the Lord's Prayer; The Creed and the Ten Commandments; his nipples serving as punctuation marks for the twenty-third psalm. His arms depicted an assortment of emotions from amorous hearts and Cupid's bows to bloodstained daggers and the Skull and Cross-bones. I suppose that the catalogue of female names was a record of his past successes and disasters. He was also an alcoholic but nevertheless a pleasant man who always removed his pipe from his mouth when speaking to the clergy!

Six uniformed matelots carried the departed sailor to his last port of embarkation. With great solemnity and with thoughts of a special rum ration awaiting them they laid the coffin on the catafalque. At the appointed moment of no return I pressed the dispatch button. He should have sailed away into the sunset or more correctly into the waiting incinerator but nothing happened. I pressed a second time without result. I kept the button depressed.

The crowded congregation looked on.

I didn't know that the manual mechanism had broken down.

Then from the curtain which covers the aperture to the

waiting chamber appeared a hand.

Slowly and stealthily it groped forward along the side of the cofin and exposed a grimy, tattooed arm. This pictorial limb explored the coffin until it made contact with a brass handle. Gripping this firmly the hand pulled the coffin through the curtains at a speed that was unnerving. It went through broadside on.

At least Cinders had shown initiative!

Gutsy

Funerals are great occasions for feeding. In the North there are actually 'professional funeral goers'; those who scan the deaths columns in the newspapers.

'I see Maggie; there's a funeral at Jesmond. That's a good place for a meal; let's do that one today!'

I was conducting a cremation. The little chapel could not contain all the mourners.

'Bob,' I said to the undertaker, 'What a crowd. He must have been well liked.'

'Not necessarily. He lived at Cambois.' [this is pronounced as 'Cammus'].

'What's that got to do about it?' I asked in ignorance of the deep ties of blood and friendship in that close-knit pleasant community.

'Well, when there's a baptism, wedding or funeral, everybody turns up,' said Bob.

'Will they all go back to the house for the funeral tea?'

'Most assuredly,' assured Bob, 'I've seen the bathtub!'

'What's a bathtub to do with it? Do they have ablutions before eating?'

'No; nothing like that. The zinc bathtub that miners wash in and which usually hangs behind the kitchen door, is filled with pease pudding on occasions like this. As the mourners go back to the house they pick up a ladle, scoop a ladleful of pease pudding on to their plates, then select a slice of boiled ham; sometimes cooked before the death in preparation, and take a slice of sly cake.

'I've heard people who were not satisfied say "That was a mean funeral. The sly cake was so sly you never even saw it!" ' Bob told me.

I had to conduct the burial of an old lady who died aged one hundred and one and four months! It was a great feast!

Her brothers and sisters were there and equally as ancient. After we had eaten, one of the brothers said, 'Let's do our party pieces!'

They were already in party mood for they'd given me a mug to drink from. I had an initial difficulty until I discovered that it was an old fashioned moustache cup with a kind of protective sieve near the lip. When I had drained the cup a ceramic bullfrog gaped at me from the bottom

According to the brothers' wish we all did 'our party piece' and a jolly good time was had by all! The old folks danced and the younger ones, in their mere seventies sang or recited. Good old granny had a splendid send-off.

I had a meal at a home when I went to arrange a funeral but it seems as if the dead man had forestalled me.

'You know, vicar, the grave is hungry.'

I didn't know!

'Just before he died Tom asked for fish and chips. We sent out for some and he ate a double portion. Then he asked for grapes; black grapes. I had difficulty in buying them as none of the shops seemed to have them.'

'Where did you get them from?'

'I had to go to the market. He ate every grape and the stalks too!'

'Well,' said I, 'he was well nourished for his journey.'

'Draw up your chair and have something to eat yourself, vicar,' I was invited.

I was ready to eat but especially to drink as it was a stifling hot day and there was a huge coal fire burning in the grate. Perspiration poured down my spine.

I drew up but couldn't get my legs under the table. I lifted the table cloth to discover to my horror that the dead man's coffin was being utilized as a table. It put me off my food. I couldn't help thinking of those chips and grapes.

That was a posh funeral; they had Black Forest gateau and china cups.

The biggest meal that I have ever eaten was prior to a funeral and while the man was still alive and kicking; very much kicking. He was a professor of science. He had lost his only son in a bus crash and soon after that his wife had died. In solitude his mind began to deteriorate. I called on him.

'Hello, Jan,' I greeted him as he answered the doorbell of his attractive wooden bungalow, set in truly sylvan surroundings. He was a Dane.

'Do come in, vicar; I'm delighted to see you. Make yourself comfortable. I was just going to have a meal. You must have some with me.'

It was six o'clock in the evening.

I followed him into the larder. Hanging from a hook was a ham shank. It was popping with maggots; large, bloated maggots! He took it down and began to cut slices from it; many slices as if he was expecting to feed an army.

'I don't think I'll have any ham, Jan,' I remarked. I was a coward and thought that the maggots might give me worms.

'Nonsense,' he said 'you must have some. We'll have eggs with it.'

When he brought me my plate it was covered with slices of fried ham and four eggs. He provided an excellent wine.

With great difficulty and under strict scrutiny I managed to stuff myself with all those victuals. I sat back exhausted.

'But you must have more', said Jan.

Slices of ham and four more eggs later I began to feel my stomach reacting.

'But some more,' he insisted. He was keeping pace with me.

'I really couldn't,' I tried to insist.

His mood turned ugly.

'You'll eat up what I give you!'

So another plateful. Then when I was feeling really sick he collapsed.

I phoned the doctor. He came round immediately and Jan was carted off to hospital. There were only four mourners at his funeral; not enough to justify a meal. Anyhow, I didn't fancy food right then!

In much happier circumstances I was challenged to eat a big meal. I was in Genoa. The commander and I were having afternoon tea on the roof of a sixteen storied hotel. The scenery was magnificent. An orchestra sat on the dais but did not play. When the waiter brought the bill he placed it before the commander who by sleight of hand transferred it for my perusal.

'Hey, Joe,' I called the waiter.

Expecting a tip he hurried towards our table.

'What's all this? Coffee and cake so much and extras double that amount. We haven't had any extras!'

'Yes, sir, you pay for the band!'

'But the band hasn't played,' I objected.

'It's their rest time!' he replied.

'And we don't subsidise their bait time. If you want this bill paid get them to get off their backsides and play something.'

So we were treated to practically every composer I know!

'I heard you speak,' said a stranger at another table,' and correct me if I'm wrong but you must be a Geordie.'

'Near enough,' I agreed.

'My name is Paul, Paul Burlando and I come from Gateshead.'

So we began a most pleasant conversation and it ended with his invitation to dinner.

'I'll bet you cannot eat the steak,' he declared.

'Why not? Is it tough?'

'Far from it. It will be so big. How about it. If you cannot finish you pay for the meal.'

I would eat a mountain of garbage rather than pay so I took the bet.

I purposely refrained from having an entrée but when the steak was served I gasped. It must have come from an elephant. I've never seen such a steak. I struggled with it. I did physical exercises half way through it; went for a walk towards the end but finally had to admit defeat. So did the commander. We lost our stake-money! I'll place my bet on a good funeral nosh-up at any time!

Nothing to endow

The bows of H.M.S. *Hydra* reared and plunged like a stricken yet determined seahorse as it ploughed its way through the turbulent waters of the northern seas. The grey February morning scarcely lifted the wet blanket of night. We did not have much armament as we were an assault ship working with Combined Operations but our guns' crews and look-outs were closed up; to the landlubber they were at their stations. It was absolutely necessary for a torpedo had been fired at us. We executed a dramatic ninety degrees turn to starboard to avoid it while we awaited a second attack. This did not materialise and it was considered that the attacking U-boat must have been returning from the Atlantic and had already expended all her torpedoes save one! Lucky for us.

'Hands muster on the seamen's messdeck midships for morning prayers.'

The bosun's shrill piping reminded us that although there was a war it was still Sunday in the Royal Navy.

'Will you conduct prayers, Lieutenant Richardson?' asked the captain.

We did not carry a chaplain and I was considered to be a 'God-botherer'!

After our intercessions the captain stood forth.

'I publish the banns of marriage,' he began, exercising his authority, 'between John Richardson, bachelor of this ship and Ethel Morallee Fawcett, spinster.'

Then he continued according to ecclesiastical and Admiralty requirements;

'If any one knows any cause or impediment why these two persons may not be lawfully joined together in holy matrimony you are to declare it; not to me but to the First Lieutenant who will be pleased to receive your objections.'

Eight weeks and three thousand nautical miles later I was on my way home there having been no objections raised onboard although I had received a very mixed bag of advice. If I had followed all the graphic counselling that both officers and ratings gave me I would have entered a monastery!

The Admiralty had drafted me from my ship to duties at the Admiralty so I had ten days' leave. I had all my worldly goods with me, as I travelled by train, ready to endow. They were a little impoverished as I had squandered money on presents for the bridesmaids and best man. I had cash in the inner pocket of my greatcoat to squander further while on honeymoon in the silver city by the sea, Aberdeen.

Just before midnight the train pulled into Newcastle station. The blue lights required by blackout regulations made the place look eerie and figures indistinct. I thought it was a Nazi but in fact it was a porter who might have been one.

'Porter, please help me with my luggage,' I requested.

He had a ridiculous little moustache and what I took to be jackboots. His voice was gutteral and insolent.

'I'm due off at eleven and it's well past that now. Look after your own luggage!'

'Heil Hitler!' I shouted at his receding figure. Was he goose-stepping? No other porter materialised out of the blue gloom. I found a trolley and loaded on to it my officer's tin trunk, a fully expanded Revelation suitcase and two other cases and my greatcoat.

Beyond the ticket barrier I espied an RAF officer who I knew rather casually.

'Hello Roger; do you know if the last train for home has left yet?' I asked.

'I wouldn't know,' he replied, 'I'm not going home.'

'Would you mind keeping an eye on my trolley here while I go and ask the ticket collector? Won't be a minute.'

'O.K.; Roger and out,' said this newly commissioned officer.

'Hello, Jack; on leave again?' greeted the ticket collector even though I had not been home for almost a year, 'when do you go back?'

So we chatted for a moment.

'You'll have to get a taxi; the last train to your place has gone,' was the encouraging reply. 'How much leave are you having?'

'I'm getting married tomorrow; then ten glorious days!' I said.

'You know my advice then? Start how you intend to finish; show her who's boss!' he laughed and then on an urgent note exclaimed, 'Isn't that your luggage?'

I turned. A man in khaki uniform was casually walking

away with my loaded trolley, so casual in fact that I really thought that he had made a mistake.

'Hey!' I yelled 'that's my luggage.'

He never turned round but began to run. Would-be passengers made way for him.

'Stop thief!' I shouted repeatedly and would have caught up with the miscreant had not a huge, dirty boot not stuck itself out from the crowd to bring me flat to the ground. I didn't like the taste of a station forecourt especially when it was mingled with blood from my own nose!

'Now, now, what's all this?' It was like a pantomime! The L.N.E.R. police sergeant peered down at me, 'What are you doing down there?'

'Kissing the deck! Quick, someone's stealing all my gear; he's got my trolley. Get after him!'

'What's your name and regiment?' asked the custodian of the law.

'Never mind that. Let's get after the thief.'

A red-capped military policeman now hove in sight from the blue darkness of the station.

'Having a spot of trouble, sergeant?' he asked.

I exploded. I dashed in the direction that had been taken by the thief chased by the two rather irate police officers. It was useless. The bird had flown.

'Don't worry,' said the railway man, 'We'll close all exits.'

They must have left the entrances clear for the quarry escaped. The next morning with no ready cash but a cheque book I entered the jewellers' shop. He was correctly dressed in a black jacket and striped trousers. He peered over his glasses at me.

'You wanting something?'

'Yes, a ring.'

'Signet, engagement, wedding or ear, sir?'

'A wedding ring, please and I would prefer a twenty-two carat gold ring.'

'Can't do that sir. Don't you know there's a war on? There are limitations and the best that I can do for you is twelve carat.'

'Yes I know there's a war; I'm rather involved in fact. I've been robbed! All that I had including the ring. I'm getting married this afternoon.'

'I'm really sorry for you and the best that I can manage for you is eighteen carat,' he said, 'and that will have to be from under the counter as it were.'

'Dig a little deeper and make it twenty-two,' I implored, 'I'm in the Royal Navy and have just come back from the Atlantic.'

I might as well have just come back from the dead for all the impact I made.

'Pity; I bought the engagement ring from this very shop,' I said.

'Did you, sir? Well, that makes all the difference. Must

look after old customers. Twenty-two it is. Would you care to make any further purchases; for the bridesmaids for example?' I felt like putting a ring through his nose!

I stood alongside the bride in church and in a borrowed shirt after a shave with a borrowed razor. The bruise was showing on my nose.

Then the crossing of the Rubicon!

'Wilt thou have this woman to thy lawful wedded wife?'

I had been warned. To respond in a meek whisper would encourage the dear old ladies in the congregation to consider me to be under the complete domination of my wife; henpecked! On the other hand, to be too bold in answering would brand me as a wife-beater! So with a modulated yet firm voice I said those fateful words, 'I will.'

'Not yet!' exclaimed the rector, 'there's more to it; Wilt thou...'

I found myself plighting my troth; love, comfort, honour and maintenance through health and sickness.

'Now,' said the rector.

'I will,' almost inaudibly from the side of my mouth.

Two rings. 'I will' twice!

'Sure to have twins' mused the sages.

I endowed Ethel with all the goods that were not now mine. The dowry was nil; not even a milking cow or a billy goat!'

I was a proper goat at my reception. I made the worst speech I have ever made. My excuse? I was off balance; but so is every groom!

It was not quite as bad as the speeches at a wedding I had just solemnised. The groom was a barrow boy who sold 'seconds!' The bride worked in the school kitchens. I sat next to the bride's uncle. He kept rabbits and kept me well informed of the breeding habits of the wee creatures.

The meal was over and it was now the appointed time for toasts and speeches. None appeared to be forthcoming.

'The bride's father ought to propose the health and future happiness of the happy couple,' I remarked to the uncle.

'Leave it to me; I'll inform the best man,' said the uncle.

The best man was busy drinking at the bar so the uncle whispered into the ear of the bride's father.

He was about to stand up when the bride's mother, a virago of thirteen stones, picked up a carving knife and said, 'We haven't cut the cake yet. Where's the bridegroom?'

'Gone to the toilet,' said someone.

'Go and get him out,' commanded the old battleaxe as she gave her daughter a sympathetic look as much as to say 'I told you so!'

There was a delay of ten minutes because the groom had not been in the toilets but had been chatting up a young female guest outside. He came in to face the undisguised ire of his future mother-in-law! The cake was cut. The mother informed everyone that she had baked it. I requested a small portion with no cement on it!

Then the bride's father stood up.

'Everybody; here's to them,' and he fell back into his chair to be kissed by the bride who had kissed almost every other male in the room. It was her day!

The groom rose unsteadily. I don't know whether it was fear or beer. Guests gave him a rousing ovation and one yelled 'It will soon be tonight!'

'Thanks,' he said and sat down.

The best man got to his feet.

'If anyone wants to see the wedding presents they are at Maggie's house,' and he sat down.

The uncle then said to me, 'I feel that I ought to say something. I'm the girl's godfather.'

'Splendid,' I recommended.

He levered himself upright and began:

'Bride and bridegroom, parents of both sides, ladies and gentlemen and of course, Reverend sir...'

'Ah,' I thought, 'this man knows what it's all about.'

'I won't say much as all the previous speakers have said all the things that I was going to say. Good luck to them!'

I was in time for the soccer results and a cup of coffee by

the fireside!

In the same church I was officiating at another marriage.

'Therefore if any man can shew any just cause why they may not lawfully be joined together, let him now speak or else hereafter for ever hold his peace.'

'I object!'

There was a deathly hush. Not a pregnant hush as the bride was mature. All would hear the clear, distinct words of the distinguished looking gentleman who stated the objection. The gathered guests turned their heads as if automatically towards him. Some sniggered behind their hands. The organist found the lost chord and the ladies of the choir almost broke their necks as they strained forward to miss nothing.

'Come with me to the vestry, please,' I invited the objector and the bridal party.

'Now; can you explain. Is your objection sound and reasonable?'

'Yes, sir. I am a solicitor and I object to this marriage on behalf of the bridegroom's wife. She is sitting in the church.'

'How did she get to know?' asked the groom who had spent weekdays with the bride and weekends with his wife.

Another groom was checking the marriage registers with me in the vestry prior to his marriage. Two strangers came in from the churchyard.

'We are detectives, vicar. If this man goes ahead with this marriage we will have to arrest him on a charge of bigamy.'

'Oh, Hell,' said the groom as his Paradise was lost and he left by the vestry exit.

'The bride's waiting in the church porch, vicar. Are you ready?' asked the verger.

Am I ever?

Weekend

'Saturday morning; the luxury of a lie-in!' I yawned.

'Not so easy, Jack,' warned Ethel, 'It's today that they judge the gardens.'

'What time?'

'I don't know but it all depends on where they begin; you'd better get up,' advised Ethel.

'I'll just have five minutes more,' I procrastinated.

Half an hour later I awoke. The sun was drying the dew from my recently transplanted flowers, (I was cheating a little!) I struggled into my socks; cut my chin to shreds in a hurried shave and spilt my coffee! I needn't have hurried; the judge arrived in my garden at four p.m. She was lovely. Her hat had more flowers adorning it than there were in my garden. She was cheating too; they were all artificial and left-overs from Ascot. She looked like a perambulating Hanging Garden of Babylon!

I reckoned that God knew a thing or two about gardens for He has called Heaven Paradise which simply means a garden. But even He did a bit of cheating; He put Adam and Eve in to do the work; to dress it and keep it. So I offered up a wee prayer but I began to read the writing on the wall when she donned a pair of dark glasses. She had judged all the other gardens and had come to mine last.

Dazzled by its beauty, staggered by the depth of thought put into it (less than a spade deep!) she must have recognised it immediately as a winner.

This placed her in a quandry. She had seen the mediocre efforts of the competitors and had tossed up a coin to make her decision. Now she must retract! Faced with a galaxy of beauty, the meticulous neatness and the gentle hum of the honey bees as they avoided my flowers she knew instinctively that the ultimate prize must be mine.

But I must maintain goodwill towards the church and her clergy. I must not alienate any waverers by defeating them in the horticultural field. So I begged her; pleaded with her; fell on my knees upon the velvet, well trimmed lawn edged with exotic plants and supplicated that she bore in mind the honest efforts of my rivals and award the prize in their direction. Also in order to eventually walk in the garden of the life to come I wished to remain humble and not be puffed up with pride, even if it was justifiable pride!

They agreed reluctantly but to ease their troubled consciences they awarded me a plaque for 'endurance and faith' and a book entitled, *How to Cheat at Gardening!*

I sought consolation in religion. After giving the morning congregation hell-fire, weeding them out and consigning them to the eternal compost heap, I mellowed to conduct baptisms in the afternoon. After all, here were God's little seedlings which the church must succour and shelter from the cruel winds of evil.

'My daughter is bringing her daughter home to be baptised.'

'Where from?' I asked.

'Africa; the dark continent!'

'She's a trifle young to come all that way,' I suggested.

'The doctor said it would be alright.'

'Which doctor?'

'That's right!' responded dear old granny.

So when the baby arrived at church clad in a grass skirt and with a bone through its nose I reached for the Service of baptism amended according to Ju-ju practices; Rite Hoodoo.

There were other recipients of this initiating sacrament. The grandfather of one had, like me, a twin sister. He was a kitchen outfitter tycoon. I had been stuck in the kitchen for years slaving over a hot stove or a steaming sink so I bore him a certain amount of malice. The baby had five godparents who had brought with them gifts from kitchen sinks to fitted units. However I rather think that there was an air-lock in his plumbing causing a slight overflow.

I had a sherry and cake to fortify me for the evening service. As I walked through the village which was preparing for the tidy-village contest I saw a floral display opposite to the vicarage. In golden flowers it read, '1788 – 1988'.

This puzzled my mind all through the service. What had happened in 1788? I flew to my encyclopedia; 1788 – nowt!

Could it be purely local? How long had the vicar been here? Was it the bicentenary of the first settlers in this Northumbrian outpost? Ah, without knowing it I had touched the correct reason. It was the bicentenary of the first settlers in Australia but what that had to do with this village I did not know!

Later that evening I went to the old people's home for an evening prayer and hymn singing.

They have a piano. Not an ordinary piano by any means

and it is older than any resident in the home. It has been wonderfully and tastefully renovated. It has three lids! One lid lifts; another slides and the third pushes. Can it play? Magnificently if Eva the pianist would hit the right keys. It was at one time played by the Queen of Denmark. A long time ago the royal House of Denmark had a remote relative who became a resident at this old folks' home. Hard to believe but still absolutely true. In appreciation of the kindnesses shown towards the royal old lady her Queen gave the home this splendid piano. It bears a small plaque which tells the circumstances of the gift. Eva knocks seven bells out of it every Sunday but it's a great Dane!

Walking towards my car after the hymn singing I met a dear old lady.

'Good evening,' I greeted her.

'Hold out your hand,' she responded in a sing-song voice. I did.

She studied it and then in melodious notes sang, 'Never done a hard day's work in its life!'

Maybe she was right; but one ought to see the callouses on my brain!

Flogging a dead horse!

THOU SHALT...

The commandment thundered, not from the awesome heights of Sinai amid lightnings and earthquakes but from the highest Episcopal throne in christendom; Durham.

Were we, the diocesan clergy to turn our backs on the world, the flesh and the devil? Were we to begin a session of soul bashing, scourging our sinful selves and walk through the wilderness of self denial and mortification of the flesh? Not at all! The path that we were called to follow was indeed the very opposite. 'Thou shalt go...to Butlins'

Holiday Camp, Filey!'

The Bishop in his unfathomable reasoning and profound wisdom decreed it would be good, indeed necessary, to gather his minions for a combined retreat and conference in such stimulating surroundings. Wives and sweethearts were not to accompany!

'Wide is the gate that leads to perdition'. The world; the flesh and Satan enticed us from within those gates. There were pretty lights and pretty girls as I suppose there are in Heaven; dance floors and recreation spaces also have their counterpart in Paradise where one can harp and dance through Eternity on fleecy clouds but roulette wheels and

betting shops have yet to be installed among the delights that await us. In the warm weather, the resultant garments (I refer to the camp and not to the Hereafter) displayed much of the flesh; the devil seemed active in extra-mural activities and the world abounded in the mammon of money and merchandise!

Our Rural Dean, uncomfortably perched on a stage winged by twelve feet high nudes, mermaids and appropriately a flight of overfed cherubs, addressed us as we gathered there for our first session.

'We will meet in, and use for our lectures, the Kent dining room. We will rig a church there for services which will be unrigged after each service. Today we will meet there after the campers have had their tea and before our tea we will say evening prayers. You will then be free until nine tonight when we must meet again for compline and to meet our lecturers.'

'What about supper?' I dared to ask. The flesh was prevailing.

'A list of clergy mealtimes will be posted on the main notice board.'

'Good morning, happy campers; wakey-wakey! Another bright morning; rise and shine!'

The tannoy system aroused the campers but disturbed our devotions. During our morning session of lectures the same happy campers wearing paper hats which bore invitations to such worldly activities as 'Kiss me quick', peered in amazement through the large windows at the sombre, dog-collared collection of clerics.

My main friend and companion was a rector called Ron; a rebel!

'I'm not attending the evening session. I've had enough of this. What about you, Jack?'

I fell to the Tempter; 'There's a good film at the cinema tonight.'

We both entered the toilets not for the relief of any natural hazard but to avoid the hazard of perhaps meeting the Bishop before he had got to the evening lecture. We concealed ourselves in separate cubicles. Just when we thought that it was safe to emerge we heard voices. The Bishop was conversing in the toilet with a camp official. Surely my Lord Bishop was not dodging the evening talk and following us to the delights of the silver screen! They talked long enough to create anxiety in Ron.

'Oh, Bishop, you blabber; shut up and get cracking. We'll miss the main feature,' groaned Ron in a hoarse whisper to me across the partition. The Bishop couldn't have heard but perhaps there was a sympathetic thought transference. He left!

So did we, for the cinema. The lights were low as we crept in. After the first reel of film the lights came up. Pretty sales girls were spotlighted with their trays of cigarettes, ices and goodies but the lights also revealed that half of the cinema audience were men and all suffering from sore throats or afraid of infection as they sat with their jacket collars turned up to hide their dog-collars!

It is just as well to be hung for a sheep as for a lamb so when the film show was over Ron and I decided to go to the theatre to watch what remained of a variety show. As we slunk on a low keel, past Kent dining room we could see pious parsons listening to a prattling prelate and our hearts were filled with pity for them.

On the stage Merlin the Wonderman performed. His star-spangled, conical hat found symmetry in his silver pointed beard. Taurus, the bull, jostled with Leo the lion on opposing breasts of his long astronomical garment which would have made a good nightshirt for Patrick Moore, that is if Patrick ever sleeps at nights.

Merlin's assistant moved among the audience like an elephant on tip-toe. She was old hen made up as chicken; mutton dressed as lamb. Superfluous flesh oozed from her scanty costume making her appear like a perambulating, over-full rubber tree! There was no room on her attire for a galaxy of stars but a crescent moon struggled to rise against her pelvic bulge.

'What is the number of this one pound note?' she asked

the mystic Merlin as she took a note from the wallet of a man in the audience.

'G over 94,620012, and it's issued by the Royal Bank of Scotland.'

Quickly the Aberdonian retrieved the note and returned it to the moth-ridden depths of his sporran.

The blindfolded Merlin was then asked, 'What have I in my hand?'

'A watch.' Maybe he could hear it ticking!

'What time does it give?'

'It's ten minutes fast!'

Impressive stuff!

She came alongside me. Not only did her flesh ooze; her body odour did with the overpowering scent of a stable. I kept my hand over my money and hid my watch.

'Ask him what is happening in Kent dining hall,' I requested. She passed on quickly.

Removing his blindfold Merlin did a commercial.

'I read the future. I can tell yours. My consulting room will be open every day. Drop in and see what the future holds for you.'

The following afternoon, having endured a homilly on how to manage bereavement while happy campers gambolled and frolicked full of life beside the nearby pool Ron and I decided to meditate between the one-armed bandits and the contest for the most glamorous granny.

'Hey, there's Merlin's place,' exclaimed Ron. It was a whitewashed, plastered hut.

'Why don't you go in, Ron?' I asked, 'You're keen on that kind of stuff.'

He pondered.

'Let's toss for it,' he suggested. I lost so went in. One pound was a lot of money in those days so I expected much. Merlin was screened from a waiting area by a night-sky curtain. On the table stood a crystal ball, a pack of tarot cards and a plaster cast of a cranium bisected by so many numbered lines that it looked like a butcher's guide to meat cuts.

'Ah, sit down, sir.'

I sat. I was wearing an open necked sports shirt and grey slacks. He passed a mug across to me. It was badly chipped and heavily stained. 'Have some tea,' he invited. The mug made me feel sick!

'No thanks.'

'Come on; it's a warm day; good for a drink of good old char.'

'No, I never drink tea,' I responded truthfully.

'Surely not. Come on; you've drunk out of worse than this when you were in the army,' he insisted without avail.

I had been in the navy but I didn't enlighten him. He then began to ask me questions about myself. I didn't reply. He thought me dumb! Failing to elicit any information about me he began his fortune-telling exposition.

'Look into the crystal ball.'

I peered.

'The mist is clearing; look carefully. What can you see? he asked.

'Myself upside down.'

He was not amused.

'You are a chargehand in a garage,' he began, 'but there is a change in store for you very soon. The foreman is to be fired and you will be promoted. You will move home to above the premises. Am I right so far?'

'You could be,' I replied.

'Life will be made difficult for you by an employee who thinks that he should be the foreman. Get rid of him as soon as you can.'

He paused; I grinned. He was encouraged.

'You have two children.'

'No. I have three.'

'Not at all; only two,' he insisted.

'Well, I had three when I came here,' I asserted.

'No, you didn't.'

'Yes I did.'

'You only thought that you had three. The last one is not yours. Your wife is having an affair with an Air Force officer but you probably suspect that. Is she with you at this camp?'

'No!'

'Have you asked yourself why not?'

'I know why not,' I replied, 'and I also know that you are an old fraud!'

I spoke very loudly so that waiting customers beyond the dividing curtain could hear me.

'Sssssh; be quiet,' he begged, 'aren't you satisfied?'

'I'm satisfied alright. Satisfied that you know nothing. You're a charleton. I'm not a garage chargehand and never have been!'

'What are you, then?' he asked.

'It was up to you to tell me, but I'll tell you. I'm a clergyman.'

He was amazed. 'You should have told me. You see it is not possible to tell a clergyman his fortune.'

'I want my pound back.'

He almost died of apolexy; he hadn't foreseen that.

'Alright, keep it and use it towards getting a correspondence course on pelmanism.'

Wednesday was sporting day. The Bishop arranged a cricket match between the clergy and the happy campers. Clergy were conscripted not only as players but as spectators too. Ron and I lay on the grass. We had a small, transistor radio. It was also Derby day.

'Fancy a flutter on the gee-gees? A tanner each way won't break you,' said Ron.

'I know nothing about racehorses,' I informed Satan's advocate.

'Well, here's the paper. Choose one you fancy and let's disappear to the betting shop as quickly as possible.' Ron was determined.

'We'll be missed.' I was faint-hearted.

'They'll think we've gone to the toilets; choose a cuddy!'

There was only one grey horse running in the race and its name was Battleship. Its odds were twenty-five to one.

'That's the one for me,' I declared confidently, 'A sure

winner.'

I had lost on Merlin; I felt sure that I would sail home on Battleship!

The radio was concealed beneath a rug and toned down. The Bishop moved among us like a saboteur. He was standing too near to us as the Derby runners came under starter's orders.

'Excuse me, your Lordship, I cannot see the batsman,' said Ron who disliked watching cricket. With ecclesiastical dignity the prelate paraded past us. The horses were off too, but only four were to finish the course. Never before in the history of the race had such a thing happened. A horse fell; it's a flat race! Other horses fell over it. There was a pile up. The original faller had to be destroyed; its name was Battleship; scuttled at Epsom. The following day I saw a queue alongside the betting shop.

'What are they doing?' I asked Ron.

'Collecting their winnings,' he answered.

'Hang on a minute,' I said as I sprinted faster than Battleship towards the betting shop. I joined the queue. I reached the pay-out window and presented my betting slip. The clerk perused it.

'This is no good. That horse was shot. You get no winnings.'

'I haven't come for winnings,' I retorted, 'I've come for compensation!'

The next Sunday we were all back in our pulpits.

Broth

I have a capacity for getting into the soup! Embarrassments have been manifold. I dare not tell the worst! Like the time when I was in Malta and the Royal Marines gave a party, or when I was taking part in a nativity play. NO! I must resist the temptation. The ingredients of my soup are TRUTH, although portions of this may be hard to swallow; HUMOUR, like animal crackers; and EMBROIDERY, just a sprinkling, like herbs, to disguise the soup pan and the consumers!

I am sitting in my cottage overlooking the farmyard. It is pouring with rain which ideally should be clear soup but having penetrated the pollution of our air now hits the deck. The deck is the farmyard which has a liberal supply of slurry and silage and quite a carpet of beefstock left by the passage of over two hundred milking cows. The rain mixed with the aromatic ingredients of the farmyard results in a thick, slimy soup.

Now I offer you a pan of mixed soup, perhaps a thick broth, for your sampling reminding you of the main ingredients of truth; humour and embroidery.

The postman always rings twice; but not in the country! He opened my door and yelled, 'A package for you!' He came right in. I was having my breakfast while still attired in my pyjamas.

'Sit down. Have you time for a coffee?' I asked.

'Yes, but I feel that it should be champers!' he replied joyfully.

'Why?'

'After all these years my wife is pregnant. There'll be a job for you next year,' said the excited postie as he sipped at his coffee. 'Just found out yesterday.'

'Well, whatever it is put its name down on the housing list straight away,' I advised.

The package was a dog-cover for the back seat of my car. There was an 'Open now – urgent' document from the Reader's Digest offering me a fortune if I won their 'greatest ever' contest. The electricity bill wouldn't wait until I had won any contest. There was an invitation to address the Bankers' Wives High Interest Group and the offer of a free portable telephone if I took out additional insurance.

'Here's a queer one for you,' said the postman perusing a

postcard printed in purple ink, 'It's an invitation to an open day at an undertakers' premises.'

'Let's see it,' I requested, 'It must be a lark!'

'Aye, well, it must be a dead one!' quipped the postman.

Sure enough it was an invitation to an open day at a funeral director's new premises.

'You'll have to take your body along,' laughed David the postman, 'But make sure that you get a return ticket!'

'What on earth can we do at an undertakers?' asked my wife.

'No doubt we'll relax in the chapels of rest; try out a few empty boxes for size and have a slow ride round the cemetery in a hearse. I think we should go. It'll be unique and besides, it offers refreshments,' I suggested.

We went.

True to north country tradition there was an ample supply of pease pudding, boiled ham and currant slab known up here as sly cake. It's so sly, one is lucky to get a bit! Whisky, coffee and tea were also available. The coffee and tea were still available after the visit was over!

Floral tributes stood in every corner and the hearse gleamed so as to reflect the wreaths and floral sprays. The chapels of rest invited one to lie down but we missed out on a visit to the 'Treatment' room. We were afraid there would be a demonstration.

Driving home again (thankfully), I remarked to my wife, 'I'd better accept the Bankers' wives' invitation to speak. Might help my overdraught!'

'You'll get your dinner at least. What'll you speak about?'

'I'll draft a few notes of interest,' I replied.

I did get a dinner. The main course was alleged game pie! I sat next to my own bank manager's wife.

'See those black bits in your pie? It's hedgehog!' I teased.

'Hedgehog? But surely hedgehog isn't game,' she objected.

'In this hotel it is!'

'I'm not going to eat it,' she decided.

I did. I was ill for four days.

The undertaker's canvassing for business bore fruit if that's what they call a corpse. An aquaintance of mine became the temporary tenant of a chapel of rest.

His vicar invited me to participate in the funeral service. The vicar was called Thrush; he was a queer bird. He had started his adult employment as a fish porter on North Shields quay. He saw the light in a miraculous draught of fishes which had escaped the eagle eyes of the Common Market commissioners. After his ordination he had served a short service commission with the army. He left before his time had expired; there was something fishy about it!

We began our slow procession up the churchyard path, preceding the coffin.

'I am the resurrection and the life,' began the vicar with stentorian decibels and showing his irritation at the flies attracted to his hair dressing; fish oil no doubt!

We reached the church doors. They were shut. We stopped. The vicar startled stained glass saints as he shouted, 'We brought nothing into this world...and you'll soon be out of it if you don't open this b----- door.'

I'm sure that the fishing fleets out in the North Sea could hear him. The verger inside did and shouted back through the solid oak door, 'The bolt's stuck.'

'Kick the b----- thing.' One would think that he had cut himself while gutting fish. 'Get someone to help you.'

'The churchwarden's helping. Hang on!'

'Hang b----- on,' intoned the vicar and the vocabulary of the foyboatmen took over so that I really cannot repeat it. My friend in the box would not mind the delay but would take grave exception to the language now being hurled about. He had served in the navy and was therefore unaccustomed to such colourful language.

'In the midst of life we are in death and I'm prepared to demonstrate the truth of that if you don't get this ------ door open.'

With a metallic clatter that could awaken the dead the door moved a little and the vicar's neat footwork completed the opening.

'The first hymn is number 275, "Brief life is here our portion",' announced the vicar. The organ began to play. The organ began to falter and smoke. The fumes were noxious. It whimpered to a stop. The organist, with flying surplice, vaulted quickly over the angelic end of a pew and sought sanctuary in the sanctuary. The electric motor had burnt out; so had the vicar. I coughed and spluttered as I took over the service. We laid my friend in his narrow bed; the vicar took to his!

A clergy deanery meeting is a thing to be avoided. Knowing that, the Rural Dean placed an obligation upon us to attend. We were to plan 'Church Unity Week'. Someone read a boring paper on 'Unity, not uniformity'. Question time was devoted to discussing who would go to what other denomination to display our fellowship. The whole thing was hypocritical but eventually all was sorted out except one.

'Will nobody go to the Pentecostal?' urged the Dean. There was a deafening roar of silence. It was if the brethren had been asked to go to a leper colony. We would have got more volunteers to go to a brothel!

'Surely someone will go,' pleaded the Rural Dean.

'I will.' They were now sure that I was a heretic.

I'm pleased that I went. It was a revelation. No one could doubt the sincerity and enthusiasm of the faithful. They expended all their energy in their worship. I wished that we could get the like in our churches.

I began my sermon.

'The sacrifices of God are a broken spirit.'

'Alleluia!' interrupted a man who had climbed on to his chair and lifted his arms heavenward, 'praise the Lord.'

'And bless the preacher,' cried a woman.

'Amen; amen,' proclaimed another.

So my sermon was punctuated by pious pronouncements and I was so carried away by this fervour that my address almost broke the time barrier.

At the close of the service we sang our fourteenth hymn of

the evening. I stood on the platform with the pastor. He was built like Mount Sion. In private life he was a printer but his hands were as large as shovels. The last line of every verse of the hymn commanded; 'Shake hands with your neighbour.'

My hand was eagerly grasped and crunched by this man-mountain. I felt my bones yield. No sooner had I sorted out my fingers than we reached the end of the second verse. Again the bone crushing exercise. There were ten verses. Alleluia!

After this episode I needed a period of recuperation. So I had a day off. Ethel, Bob the verger and Ruff my dog accompanied me to Craster on the Northumbrian coast. It was a warm day; warm enough to get kippered! After a splendid lunch we decided to walk along the mile-long seaturf towards Dunstanburgh Castle. Ruff and I walked briskly and got well ahead of Ethel and Bob. I heard shouting.

Thinking that I was too far ahead I slackened my pace but the shouting seemed to become urgent. I heard, 'Look out, Jack!'

I turned about. A bull was hurtling towards me. I dived sideways but the bull was intent and would have gored me had not Ruff taken up the challenge and tackled the bull. The bull's aggression was a lot of bull for it turned and ran! Heroics are not my sense of valour and I hurried from the scene.

We continued our outing by driving along the Border country until we reached Cornhill on Tweed. Moira served us with afternoon tea while Bob fell asleep in the hotel lounge. Ethel and I decided to continue our walking where there were no bulls. There were potholes!

Long grass hid these traps. Ethel strode manfully along until suddenly she disappeared from my view. She had gone full length upon the uneven ground.

We love walking. We had tried almost everything in order to raise money for the repair of the church roof; selling molehills at 10p each from the vicarage garden and

20p each from the consecrated soil of the churchyard; vicarage teas; antique sale; bus trips; coffee mornings and wine and cheese evenings. We still needed money.

'What about a sponsored walk?' was a welcome suggestion. A short walk around the churchyard for the elderly but a twelve mile walk for the foolhardy.

'Vicar, you plan a route.'

I did; carefully avoiding bulls and potholes.

On the day of the walk the rain never ceased. It ran down the inside of my clothing. We all began to resemble drowned rats but we plodded on through flood and torrent! I squelched along and got into a regular stride until a young labrador puppy ran to me. I stumbled. The pain from my foot ran up my leg. For a few yards I tried to continue but had to signal to the doctor who was following this senseless pack in his car. He picked me up from the flooded ditch.

'Take your boot off and let me have a look.'

There was a full tide within my boot and my sock was sodden...

'I'm afraid you've broken a toe,' he diagnosed, 'Here, take this. It mends broken toes,' and he handed me his brandy flask. I could have danced all night!

The hospital didn't prescribe brandy but they were most attentive, mainly because I had married the nursing sister and baptised her two children.

'We'd better take you to the X-ray department. Put your arm around me.' That in itself was compensation! I hobbled with her. I had also married the radiologist. They were having fun with me! Why was it necessary to have a body scan when it was my toe that was broken?

Back to the doctor who I hadn't married probably because he was a Hindu.

'There's nothing wrong with you toe. It isn't broken,' said the doctor who never removed his dark sunglasses as he examined the X-ray plates.

I hobbled out.

'Of course it's broken,' said the nurse, 'a blind man could see that.'

So today I can always be easily identified. I have a crooked toe!

Second helping

Strathill is in a triangle formed by Ashby-de-la-Zouch, Little Slaughter and Blackpool Tower. Anyway, it's in the Midlands. My first visit there is a hazy memory as I was but four years old. Even at that tender age I was adept at getting in the soup. I reckon that I must have been born with a ladle in my hand!

My maternal grandmother lived there in a quaint, ancient house. At the top of the long garden there was an outhouse built originally as a bakery for the visit of Queen Elizabeth in 1570. The house had a legion of ghosts. One was a black man who strummed a banjo while sitting on a bedroom window seat. Another, unseen, thumped anyone sitting in the lounge. Katherine de Barnes rustled her silken skirts between rooms and received wolf-whistles from a lustful phantom. Sadly all those age-old spectral residents have suffered from alleged progress as the house has now been demolished to make way for a shopping precinct. I wonder if they are at the check-outs!

We had no gas appliances at that time in our own home. Grandmother had. I turned on the gas taps and went up the garden to tease the Belgian hare in its hutch. Gran entered her kitchen. She struck a match. She lost her eyebrows! One of us, I'm not sure who it was, got stuck up an apple tree and the fire brigade had to rescue the miscreant.

The fire-fighters and their horse-drawn engine made a second visit to Granny's house the next day. It was the last evening of our visit. The twins had been put to bed early to enable my mother to go on farewell visits to her brothers and sisters. Gran breathed a prayer of thankfulness that this was our last evening there and settled in her rocking chair dozing.

Mother had bought a plentiful supply of sweets to be eaten by us when on the train homeward bound. They were left on the shelf at the foot of our bed, out of our reach!

'Make a back for me, Chris, and I'll reach the sweets,' I requested my erstwhile twin. She gave me a candlestick and knelt on all fours on the bed. I climbed and reached.

'I've got them,' I cried in my success and dropped the lighted candle.

When mother returned she found the fire brigade hosing down the bedroom and rescusitating poor old gran! We never got to eat the sweets.

I visited Strathill many years later when I was stationed at a Fleet Air Arm establishment nearby. A married-quarters house there began to belch smoke and flames from its chimney. By the time the naval fire-fighting team got there the fire had been long extinguished.

'Better make sure that there is nothing still smouldering in the chimney,' said the First Lieutenant, 'get on the roof and direct the water down the chimney.'

Harry Smith, the clerk of works and his wife were sitting quietly around their fireside in the adjoining house when suddenly a fierce jetstream of water screamed at them from their fireplace. They ran outside covered in black, wet soot and looking like grotesque, aquatic chimpanzees. The hose had been put down the wrong chimney. That is why, even today, house numbers are painted on all married-quarters chimneys!

Now I was journeying to Strathill in response to an

invitation to speak at the Mayor's civic dinner. The borough chief executive officer was chairman for the evening. He was a happy seventeen stone and had taken onboard an almost equal tonnage of alcohol. He was the embodiment of Mr Pickwick! His girth kept his mouth long distance from his dinner plate which of course he couldn't lift up like he did his glass. He had a laugh like the bellow of a bull and he was an excellent host. I sat between him and the mayor.

The borough treasurer was first to speak. He got bogged down trying to explain the virtues of the Poll Tax and in deep water endeavouring to justify the million pound construction of a swimming pool that no one wanted. Then item by item as if addressing a parliamentary board of enquiry he itemised the borough balance sheet. No one took a blind notice of him. He was so dry that the bar did a roaring business after he sat down. The mayor then murmured municipal matters and a short break was granted. It lasted forty minutes.

'Your worship, the mayor, my lords, ladies and gentlemen', there was only one lady present, 'it is my pleasure to call upon the Reverend John Richardson to speak.'

The executive officer then began to confuse everyone with a potted history of my life which even I could not recognise. I think that his secretary must have mixed files for I was presented as a cross between Mahatma Ghandi and Bob Hope! It was utter rubbish delivered in a happy, carefree manner where accuracy didn't matter. He even sited Northumberland as somewhere between the Mersey and Galloway!

When I got up to speak everyone was past caring. I 'took the mickey' out of the executive officer. He took it well. He roared with laughter and sweated pure beer.

When I sat down he said to me, 'I've never laughed so much in all my life, in fact, I've got cramp of the stomach,' and keeled over dead!

At least he died happy!

I had a much humbler meal. I was to present awards to

the nursing staff of a hospital. The nurses' dining hall was laid out specially for the V.I.P.s; one MP, senior doctors and the matron. The 'nursing student of the year' was commissioned to say Grace.

'Would you bow your heads, please, while nurse Oliver asks a blessing?' asked the presbyterian matron in her best bedside manner which brooked no refusal. Dutifully we bowed. There was a long silence.

'O God...I've forgotten it!'

She was delegated to bedpan duties for a week.

Worse was to follow. The temporary platform creaked as the matron hoisted her formidable superstructure on to it. It then took a list to starboard as the much overweight parliamentarian puffed his elevation to the other side. He wore bright red socks giving the impression he was to be next in the operating theatre. The medical superintendent and I sat midships.

I stood to present the awards.

'And now the winner of our Nightingale Trophy, Nurse Aileen Wilson!'

I couldn't believe it. Aileen made the matron look like a mere slip of a girl. She was tremendous. Her beam was that of a cruiser; her top-rigging like the Himalayas and her legs like mahogany from the rainforests. The earth trembled. I considered it best that I should go down to her but she had already commenced mounting the dais. She hesitated beside the matron and executed some kind of manoeuvre meant to be a curtsey. The MP lifted his mass to applaud and call out in good Commons fashion, 'Hear-hear.'

The platform collapsed!

The matron disappeared under a flurry of starch and linen and striped flannel. Aileen seemed to rebound repeatedly from the medical superintendent who must have needed medical attention afterwards. I was unscathed!

Events, no matter how seemingly innocent, always seem to lead me in one direction; trouble!

'Are you away now, Reverend Richardson?' asked Eddie the security man cum hall porter cum commissionaire cum general factotum. He is invaluable to the college. He knows everyone and everything.

'Is it a retirement course you're running this term?'

'Why?' I responded.

'Well, your students all seem to be well qualified for a geriatric ward. Where do you get them from, old folks' homes?'

True, some of the students seemed to qualify for that classification but Eddie must have missed the ultra-teenager who wore a small curtain pelmet as a skirt and a tight fitting sweater bearing the word 'Gullible' over her ample bosom. He mustn't have noticed the 'drop-out' whose hoary beard began where his hair straggled to an uneven end and who was an elderly eighteen years of age. Then there was the 'Merry widow' who, at twenty-one had never been married but had 'shacked-up' with numerous 'toy-boys' the first of which had killed himself! Undeterred after he was interred, she still fluttered her false eyelashes at all and sundry, changing her lovers as often as she changed her sheets. They were all studying religion!

Eddie of course was referring to my more mature students. One was a brilliant scholar in his mid seventies. He still is an outstanding man in every way; deeply religious and extremely courageous. He had lost a leg in a horrendous accident while working down the pit and the wound had never healed. He suffered yet never complained. When he left my class he was admitted to Newcastle University where at an age approaching eighty he obtained a degree!

Another mature student was a mere middle age. She was matronly and studious and being a glutton for punishment came to hear me preach one Sunday.

'Enjoy the service?' I asked her.

'Definitely,' she replied, 'but I disagreed with your sermon. You misquoted once and I thought that your exposition of eschatology was rather weak!'

My lectures were bearing fruit and I was being pruned.

'Call at my house sometime. We'll have a chat about that

and I'll give you my views on the subject. I'm inclined to believe in reincarnation,' she invited, 'I live in number thirty-two.' She was determined to teach me a thing or two!

A couple of weeks later I called on a friend and after tea was about to get into my car when I noticed a bold 32 in brass numerals gleaming from the gate opposite. Remembering my promise to call, I straightened my hair, sharpened up my intellect and rang her doorbell. She opened the door. Somehow she looked different. Her hairstyle had altered but in this age when women change not only the style of their hair but its colour whenever there's an R in the month or there's a new moon, one is never surprised. She wore a full length, tartan pinafore and as I had never before seen her in kitchen togs I reckoned that they made her appearance a little unfamiliar.

I noticed a framed photograph of a colleague who was in my term at theological college.

'I didn't know that you knew Leslie Carter,' I remarked.

'Oh, yes, he's my son's godfather. Do you know him?'

'He was at college with me in Cheshire. He and I were special friends as we had both served at sea before studying theology. Isn't he somewhere on the continent now?'

'He's in Cherbourg with the Missions to Seamen. He phones me every Friday evening,' she replied.

'It's Friday today. Will he ring tonight?'

'Almost surely, about seven o'clock.'

She began to ask me searching questions about the hereafter, punishment, forgiveness, mercy and divine understanding. Was there eternal damnation or the bliss of an understanding compassion?

I was amazed. She was not telling me all the answers that she had apparently been sure of the previous Sunday and in the classroom but seemed to be desperately searching.

'She's taking this eschatology extremely seriously. It's almost uncanny; she is so tense,' I thought to myself as I warmed to the subject.

'You've been so helpful and so clear. I really do thank you.'

Here was a most genuine and even gentle lady far from the brusqueness she so often displayed during lectures. She had listened intently.

'It's been a most invigorating and inspiring chat. It's done me good too. I'm so pleased I called,' I said.

'So am I,' she replied.

'If Leslie Carter phones you tonight give him my regards,' I asked.

'I will indeed, if you give me your name. Who are you?'

It had clearly been a case of mistaken identity. She wasn't my student but was mighty like her!

Much later Leslie told me that he had phoned her at seven o'clock and that she had passed on my message.

At eight o'clock her son came home and found her dead. She had committed suicide!

Foreseeing

The old crone sat like a bedraggled seabird upon a horizontal, wooden pile on the jetty of Alexandria harbour in Egypt.

Her face resembled the proverbial prune with more wrinkles than a corrugated iron hut. Her toothless gums impeded the intrusion of her lips into her mouth. Her hair, a woman's crowning glory, betrayed that this geriatric Cleopatra had never bathed in ass's mlk and was not likely to clasp an asp to her withered breast. Yet she was not dirty although her clothes were patched almost beyond redemption. She was pitifully thin and this accentuated her high cheekbones.

I felt that I could not pass her without some form of greeting. 'Good morning,' I said, blandly hoping that she understood English. She looked at me.

It was then that I saw her eyes!

They were noble. There was a depth of wisdom and pedigree; and inheritance of an ancient culture that embraced the ancient pharaohs including Rameses and the era of Moses. In her eyes, the windows of her soul, was a light of dignity and resignation yet mellowed with the glow of friendliness. There was pride, a virtuous pride, born of breeding and culture.

Across the bay to the east the palace of Ras el tin gleamed in the sunlight which shattered itself into a myriad of diamonds upon the quiet waters yet in this old, jetsam of womanhood I felt a greater radiance. Her eyes smiled rather than her lips. I sat beside her on that hard, uncompromising timber; she in her pitiful rags and me in my white uniform and 'Bombay bloomers'.

'Do you speak English?' I enquired.

'I speak good English because I was educated at an English school in Cyprus.'

'In Cyprus? What were you doing there?' I asked.

'Father was an English master at the school and also served in a consulate. He was a Scot married to an Egyptian lady. They had three daughters of which I am the youngest,' she began to relate in pleasing, well pronounced English.

Because of my brash youth I asked with direct boldness, 'Then why are you in such a state as I see you now?'

'The war broke out'; she was referring to the First World War.

'Father enlisted and was sent to Egypt.' She hesitated, sighed and then continued.

'He was killed. Within months, mother, who had brought us to her home in Memphis, died. For a while we existed on an ever-dwindling capital.'

Again she hesitated, 'I married. This did not work out. My husband left me for an Italian woman and I've had to exist the best way that I can.'

There was a prolonged silence broken only when she said, 'I'm a baptised Christian.' It was her turn to look into my eyes.

'You will have a change of direction in your life; a big change. Much is to happen before then. You will meet a challenge and will continue to serve but in a different way.'

'What way?' I asked.

'I don't know,' she replied, 'I can't see very much these days. I seem to be losing the sight!'

'Were you a fortune teller, then?' I enquired.

She laughed, 'Not in the sense you seem to mean, although without consciously trying I had glimpses into the future, but I kept my revelations to myself.'

Years afterwards her prediction came true. At my ordination retreat I thought of her and said a little prayer for her.

I had attached myself to the Fleet Club at Alexandria which was organised and run by the Reverend Charles Paton, RN. I also began what may be called my literary career by contributing cartoons to the Fleet magazine. Charles Paton gave the old woman, who despite her wrinkles and ageing process was barely fifty years old, employment and accommodation at the club. The last I saw of her was when she brought me a glass of orange juice as I stood at the counter of the club shop purchasing a rug. She knew that I was leaving and had come to bid me goodbye. I gave her a bible.

Changed now, as my Egyptian had foreseen, from engine room to parish room; from bilge pump to village pump and from seaside to shoreside I sat in my yet unfamiliar study at Bishopton. A hundred years previously a predecessor, Henry Ford, had 'insulated' this study against the decibels of his twelve vociferous offspring by covering the walls with sackcloth. His family had connections with the African continent. One of his sons stood on the Town Hall steps in Khartoum alongside Chinese Gordon when the latter was assassinated. On returning to his father's vicarage at Bishopton he erected a memorial to General Gordon; the very first of such in Britain.

My typewriter was a steam model, very upright as a vicar's typewriter should be but a woefully bad speller. The

'E' key never returned of its own volition after being struck and this hampered progress somewhat. The insulated walls were effective in smothering the hammering of the machine so that the rest of the house, modernised in 1700, remained undisturbed.

I had been inducted to the United Benefice of Bishopton with Great Stainton only two weeks previously. I was anxious to produce some form of parish notes; a broadsheet, before Christmas which was only two weeks away. I had purchased a folder of 'skins' or stencils. Having completed almost five pages I was left with about one third of a stencil still blank.

I was pensive, and mean. With what could I complete that page? Suddenly, as I watched the midday trek of the farmers into the Talbot Arms opposite, I too received inspiration.

For fun I would predict the number of births, engagements, marriages and removals, but not bereavements, for the ensuing year.

Many of the parishioners took my predictions seriously. One old lady pinned the sheet on the side of her tallboy and ticked off the relevant occurrences as they happened while one not so reverent farm worker had the sheet glued inside his outside lavatory. His pensive hours within that small establishment were well rewarded when at the end of that year he could emerge declaring that the vicar had been correct in his predictions. I was. I was amazed!

'Do it again for next year,' I was begged.

Anything for a lark, I laughed as I wrote down my estimates for the following year. I could scarcely believe it when they to turned out to be accurate. I began to grow not only bewildered but a little scared.

My apparent clairvoyant powers reached the national press. I think that it was the *Sunday Express* which bannered the headline, 'The second Isaiah'.

During Christmas week the phone scarcely ceased ringing. Ethel wearied. I promised to do something to end it. I deliberately doubled the numbers I first thought of thereby making the whole thing farcical.

Was it?

Not at all: I was right again.

My fame as a seer spread beyond the borders of my own wee patch to the towering high-rise obscenities, the flood-lit pylons of the centre of Saturday worship and the citadel of culture and education; the Tyne-Tees Television studios, all in the Holy City itself, Newcastle upon Tyne.

Tom Coyne was a high priest at Tyne Tees. He received an order from above instructing him to interview me on New Year's Eve. I sat with a glass of water. I studied the microbes in it before peering beyond the cameras and warming spotlamps into the future, or to be exact, into the next twelve months.

Tom made me feel at ease. He is a jovial, pleasant man and appeared to be genuinely interested in the subject of foretelling.

'Am I going to win the pools?' he asked.

I answered him accurately, 'You'll have as much chance as anyone else; ten million to one.

Undeterred, the gallant Tom, as the interview was drawing to a close, asked me, 'Now, I'll put your powers to the test. Who will win the big race tomorrow?'

Big race? What race? Was it a horse race, a dog race, a motor race, a mill race, hurdles or the human race? I hadn't a clue!

I said the first thing that came into my mind.

'No one; there won't be a race!'

Tom laughed in gentle derision.

'No race! Are you telling me that the Morpeth to Newcastle road race will not be run? It's almost a hundred years old and has always been run on New Year's Day.'

'Yes, Tom, there will be no race tomorrow!'

'Before you go have you any greeting for your parishioners?' invited Tom.

'Yes,' I replied, 'To all my parishioners both human and otherwise I wish a blessed and prosperous New Year.'

Tom queried, 'Human and otherwise? Who are the

otherwise?'

'The fairies, of course. You know that we have them at Bishopton.'

'Now come off it. I'll ask you a straight question. Do you really believe in fairies?'

What with races and the little people Tom was determined to win the day or cast a spell.

'If I said that I didn't believe in them,' I replied, 'they will kick me to death when I return home!'

That night we went to the watchnight service as it approached the bewitching hour. The graveyard yawned as we passed beneath a starlit, cloudless sky. The night air was bitterly cold and froze the three stone gargoyles on the church tower. So it was with extreme amazement that we left the church after welcoming in the New Year with praise and hope to find snow drifts piling up against the churchyard wall. With stoical fervour we did not allow this natural hazard to deter our first footing perambulations, but, for the first time in its history the Morpeth road race was postponed!

Letters began to pour in from all creeds and climes. Predictions were required for homing pigeons, surgical operations, pending matrimonial chances and financial speculation.

The most amazing letter arrived from India; the sub-continent of soothsayers, holy men and sacred cows.

13 Kyd Street
Calcutta 16
Bengal, India. 4-2-63.

Dear revd, (Sir)
This letter may be astonishing to you to receive of whom you do not know or seen at all as it is to me.

Well, sir, I was reading the Sunday Standard papers printed in Bombay dated February the 3 63 when I came across a ardtical (sic) reference to your predictions for the last five years and only one mistake.

You have stated about movements to and fro, marriages and births then about national affairs this is how I got your name.

There are a few questions to you I must ask AND RECEIVE.

1.   Could you let me know its meaning and others too. The other day about the 22nd January '63 while saying my prayers at bedside 11 p.m. During my prayers I saw a total white cross floating at eyes level a short distance away at an angle and close to left hand. The cross was on lying formation floating on water on Puffy Clouds. I still had eye shut until it disappeared.

2.   Before sometime (two days) ahead while saying my prayers in the usual way I saw a face.

3.   I do hope you will not take offend by me stating this uncalled statement pardon if so I do regret.

A few days later while sleeping I got up from sleep and could not sleep again for at least thirty minutes. The dream was such (pardon me) I saw a figure of a young girl talking to the eye. This girl came so low doing this nasty, dirty job. The girl was working as a night soil (human) remover. She came into contact with me. I asked her why she was doing this kind of work so low and why she had no covering on nose or mouth. Then to astonishment very great she opened the barrow pan, said a couple of words I not repeat to you, then to my dismay she sank the right side of her face into it then on raising it was a terrible sight to see. Here I got up. The time was about four in the morning. I enquired from those who can read palms of hands and stars and things. They told me very good to those who dream such a dream but that dreams of death, flowers, marriages and engagements are bad very bad. What do you have to say to these three items stated?

I was born in Calcutta on 8 January 1900 baptised at the old mission church Calcutta Fort William.

I belong to the high church of England...etc.
Do hope please to hear thanking you respectfully.
Have relations in England. P.T.O.

sir,

S. Whelan.

Sir, pardon me wishing a joyous Easter. Thank you.
May you and yours see many years of happiness to
come. S. Whelan.

I have written this without any editing.

I had planned a garden party at Bishopton and arranged for a fortune teller to operate. She couldn't have been much good for two days before the fete she fell downstairs and broke her leg. If she had been truly psychic she would never have gone upstairs.

This left me without a fortune teller and I had advertised that one would be there.

I was having lunch at the Missions to Seamen. Seated with me were a marine engineer, A Scot of course, a Chinese head steward, a second mate of indeterminate origin, Mary Allen the receptionist and an Indian deck officer from Calcutta.

Mary was organising a bus load of mariners and mission workers to come to the garden party. The league of nations which sat with me eating Irish stew and Manilla meringues all agreed to come. I had an inspiration. It came to me after the India wallah, called Mahatma, told us of his father.

'He is a Parsee. He is an acknowledged and professional palm reader.'

'Full time?' I asked.

'He's like you, a priest.'

'Can you read palms?' I asked the unsuspecting oriental.

'A little.'

'Then you've got yourself a job tomorrow!' I informed him. Mary urged him, I encouraged him, the others threatened him. The gaily striped tent bore the huge placard, MR X FROM THE FAR EAST.

Business boomed. According to Mahatma the baby business was to boom too. He told all the young ladies, both single and married, that they would all be pregnant before the year was out. Despite my hope for extra baptismal collections only one girl fulfilled his forecast and I officiated at her wedding two months before the baptism.

Cup Tie

'Technical College, can I help you?' asked Marie who really is most helpful. Despite all kinds of telephone calls from irritating students and irate lecturers, cantankerous councillors and the perfidious public Marie always keeps on an even keel.

'Yes, give me the cultural corner of the college, please,' I asked.

'Ah, the Reverend Richardson. You mean the library, of course. How are you?'

We had a lengthy discourse on the knitting of my broken toe which had mended like a corkscrew so that every step I took was a twist.

'I had a friend like that,' remarked the helpful Marie as the phone crackled, 'and they had to break the toe. In the end they had to amputate.'

Greatly encouraged I stood on my other foot.

'It is Bill Hume that I require,' I informed Marie.

As the phone clicked I considered life as an understudy to Long John Silver.

'Hello; library,' the sweet voice of Sylvia intoned quietly so as not to disturb the hallowed hush of that sanctified acre of meditation, study and quiet sleep.

'Jack here. Is Bill in?' I asked.

The answer took precedence over my enquiry.

'I'm going to be married, Jack,' said Sylvia.

'When?'

'I don't know, I've just become engaged.'

'Then put me through to that confirmed bachelor Bill.'

'Confirmed bachelor? In truth, no one will have him,' said the disrespectful but probably truthful Sylvia. 'Hang on.'

So it was that I arranged an interview with Bill.

I could barely discern Bill Hume's hulk that passed as a body through the polluted ozone layer and I perspired through the resultant greenhouse effect towards him. A fortune in fag-ends littered his desk obscuring any lurid pictures which lay beneath them. The walls of his office, if it can be so called as an office is normally a place of work, were plastered with illustrations, designs and photographs of vintage motor cycles with the exception of one wall. This oddment depicted relics of the Second World War surrounding a calendar displaying not only the dates but a would-be date; a two-legged Fox.

I considered Bill to be a Southerner for he hailed from County Durham yet he claimed kinship with most of the Border families. One was renowned for having supplied a Prime Minister while the others were undoubtedly Border reivers; sheep stealers and highway robbers. His ancestors danced their last waltz with a gibbet as their embracing partner.

William Elliott Douglas-Hume did not rustle cattle as he was allergic to the mad-cow disease but he was at heart a Covenantor while his lying lips professed atheism. Nevertheless he was a man one could trust so long as one could see him and his hands were in his pockets.

With a skilful anti-clockwise flick of his tongue Bill shifted his cigarette towards his left ear. His burn-scarred lips are now immune to heat but having permanently lost their moisture the cigarette paper adhered in such quantities as to give the illusion that he had papier-mâché lips.

He spoke. 'Now your reverence, what do you want?'

'How do you know that I want anything?'

He laughed. The floor trembled.

'Don't say that you've come here just to ask after my health, you lying toad.'

I was not dismayed. I recognised that he was in a generous mood but as he proclaimed a perpetual state of penury I knew that it was useless to request any monetary favour.

'Well, Bill, I need your help,' I said and then went on to explain. 'The church roof is leaking.'

'Which church roof isn't?' interrupted Bill, 'and it's due to all that dry rot that emanates from the pulpits.'

'Not in my case,' I objected. 'The roof timbers are sound. Did you know that Mitford church roof timbers came from ships that fought at Trafalgar? The salt in them is distasteful to woodworm.'

'I don't want a history lesson, you old flanneller and in any case I don't believe you,' replied the cavernous covenanter, 'You'll be telling me next that Nelson was your grandad.'

'No, but his uncle Isaac was Vicar of Mitford at the end of the eighteenth century and he died a watery death; he fell into the river after an evening in the local pub and was found drowned with a smile on his lips. O death where is thy sting?'

'I don't believe a word you say, but to get back to that church roof which seems to be as leaky as your stories,' Bill brought us back to the twentieth century.

'It's leaking like a sieve,' I exaggerated, 'and I need to raise money.'

'I might have known. Silly me for listening. Well, I'm busy just now. I wish you good scrounging. Cheerio.'

His chair groaned as he tried to stand up but I remained glued to mine.

'I'm not asking you for money, Bill,' I hastened to assure him, 'I only want your help.'

His relief acted like ballast for he sank back into his chair like a dredger bucket.

He eyed me cautiously.

'What kind of help?'

'Advice,' I replied.

His caution deepened.

'Carry on,' he said in a barely audible whisper as if he wanted me to shut up.

'How would you like to have tea on the vicarage lawn?'

'I b----- well wouldn't; Mothers' Union scones and two

teabags between fifty cups and then what would it cost me?' he protested.

'Ah, well, that's just it,' I began to explain, 'It wouldn't cost you but it would cost customers.'

Daylight began to filter into the dark recesses of his suspicious mind and with a roar like a vintage motor cycle he exclaimed, 'You're thinking of having teas on the vicarage lawn. It's a good idea.'

'On high days and holidays. How about it, Bill?'

'How about catering? You've got to make a profit,' said Bill adopting the attitude of the Listening Bank.

'That's easy. We have ladies in our working party who are not only generous but excellent cooks. There's no worry in that direction.'

'Well, what do you want me to do? I can't cook and I'm not volunteering to wash up,' remarked Bill who couldn't

recognise a tea towel or find his way into the kitchen sink.

'There's one snag,' I stated.

'There always is with you. Out with it,' said the sceptical librarian.

'We have no decent cups, saucers or plates,' I complained.

Hastily Bill removed the caffeine stained, chipped mug from his desk top to his drawer. The half cold tea in it slopped over its plimsol line to add a further ingredient to the soup stains on his trousers.

'*I've* got no cups,' he fairly bellowed.

'I can see that,' I observed, 'but you can help me to get some. I would like you to find some good pottery firms and then write begging letters to them. I only want a dozen sets.'

'You'll pay for the postage?'

'Aye,' I agreed.

'And I'll get a free tea?'

'Aye,' again.

'Agreed,' and the begging process began.

Bill wrote:

To the Advertising and Publicity Manager,
Barratts of Staffordshire.

Dear Sir,

Unblushingly and devoid of conscience I write this letter of supplication – 'begging letter' as a phrase is a little plebeian, don't you think? Anyway, I have been put on the spot and having a nasty streak inside, I cannot see any good reason why I should not make life a little difficult for others! That you should be the victim is sad but put it down to ill-luck and regard it as mortification of the spirit. Good for the soul, you know.

My personal cross is the Vicar of Mitford, one Jack Richardson, who is full of good works and dirty tricks. This likeable crook spreads sweetness and light, right, left and centre like marmalade on toast but leaves his victims empty shells of their former selves. He regards me as a scrounger of unparalleled talent (and this despite the fact that he was a naval chaplain for many years!) and has lumbered me with the acquisition of crockery so that his protégés, in and out of his blasted parish, may have communal teas on the lawn.

The mind and soul quiver.

Perhaps this is his version of mortification of the flesh. You should see some of the thugs he regards as deserving cases! In my blackest nightmares I suspect that he might have *me* in mind to aid these holocausts. One can but hope and pray.

But one must cut the cackle. He is gloating over the thought that I might be able to con the impedimenta of a tea party for a small army for him, and I am supposed to make the rounds of unsuspecting manufacturers looting stray goodies. Have you any; free or at the terrible worst, cheap? Anything from a sugar bowl to a complete service?

You laugh? Tush!

If you love me *please* deny this request. Success will only confirm the Richardson blighter's high opinion of my talents and I will be lumbered for ever!

By the way, in a streak of frenzied generosity he announced that, and I quote '...all donations will be gratefully acknowledged in the parish magazine...'

There now! Just think of the publicity.

Yours aye,

W. E. Hume.

The answer came.

April Fools' Day 1976

W. E. Hume Esq
County Technical College.

Dear Sir,

Your begging note arrived today
caused havoc in the office bay
as all and sundry left their chair
at your letter so to stare
amid amazement and disbelief.
Is it from a low-down thief?
Scrounger seems a little weak,
For the type of wares you seek
Your cross it seems is hard to bear
You seem to have more than your share
of Purging Pastors in pursuit
of anything that you can loot.
So in the cause of slight relief
have sent a parcel as beneath.
The contents should suffice the teas;
all thugs and hangers-on to please.
When sitting on the Vicar's lawn
in utter boredom gape and yawn
as Richardson beguiles the crowd
to beg and borrow neath a shroud
on his behalf and for the parish
get anything however garish.
Concern yourself not how you harass
factory types you must embarrass.
We hope Jack's future parties bring
more followers, his praises sing
and that the likes of you and yours
may give up all these tedious chores.
As in conclusion we do lend
an outstretched hand to needy friend.

As we are sure you are aware
the litter bin would be but where
a letter such as yours is put;
'Another crank or just a nut'.
To needy causes such as these
our aim; to satisfy and please.

Yours faithfully,

Barratts of Staffordshire Limited.

P.S.   A magazine would be quite nice
for later feeding to the mice
who gather round our factory floor
to relish scraps left on the floor.

The teas went down well; a gulping success.

Wood and Stone

I sat on a hard, wooden pew. Its unyielding seat flattened my posterior into an insensitive board. The numbness crept down my left leg causing spasms of cramp in my foot. The round beading which ran the length of the pew eased my fifth vertebra from its neighbour. A three pronged, five foot high, wrought-iron candlestick, which had no ritualistic significance but was the auxiliary lighting system, impaired my view of the pulpit fragmenting the preacher into a holocaust of holy relics. I watched the frustration of a wasp vainly endeavouring to disturb the composure of a stained-glass saint. Beneath that window sat a wee body wearing a true Scots bonnet and my wandering thoughts took me in the direction of Scotland and to Alva in particular from where I had recently returned. While the preacher droned on the Ochil Hills rose before my inner mind. I was reliving my first visit to Alva.

'The kirk is no' big enough,' said the minister and we want an excuse to pull it down and rebuild. Will you come and preach for us?'

They had heard that I was a devastating preacher.

Most Sassenachs, irreligious and Sabbath-profaning, regard the Presbyterian ministry to be manned by severe, austere, forbidding bigots whose main functions are to denounce enjoyment in any of its forms as frivolous and soul-destroying and to proclaim hellfire and damnation. This minister gave lie to that unwarranted theory. He is a ball of fire, not of the combustion of Hades but of life and energy. Hutton and his wife Lesley gave me a true Scottish welcome and hot chocolate at supper time.

The kirk was in immediate danger as soon as I stepped into the pulpit to preach. I thundered forth; the elders collected their seven-pound mells (hammers) and were at the ready as soon as I concluded, feeling fully justified in their acts of destruction. From that moment on the stout stone walls of the kirk began to crumble like the walls of Jericho. The front of the building was to remain but the rest had to be demolished. Instead of placing a plaque to commemorate my preaching the last sermon they razed the kirk to the ground.

On my return journey the train stopped at a small station before Linlithgow. I noticed a man cutting a length from a

piece of wood. As I watched him, still fired with holy thoughts inspired by the minister who I had last seen joyfully and wholeheartedly destroying a house of God as fervently as any atheist, and thought how noble indeed was this carpenter's work even though it was still the Sabbath day. A carpenter. Wasn't Jesus such a workman? The carpenter of Nazareth.

On returning home I received a telephone call.

'Jack; Peter here.'

This wasn't a beckoning from the Pearly Gates but the sepulchral tones of a mortician echoing down my phone.

'How's life, Peter?'

He was more interested in death. Living persons constituted a personal affront to him.

'It's not life I want to talk about! Can you do a funeral for me tomorrow?'

'I can do anyone or anything tomorrow; I'm free!' I asserted, 'but isn't it rather short notice?'

'Maybe; but you needn't worry. There'll be no one there,' Peter informed me.

'No one?' I queried.

'Well; no mourners. The only relative is the deceased's wife. She is ninety-six years old and is bedfast. They've only been up here for three months. They came home to die! You won't have to give an address,' said Peter hopefully.

I arrived at the crematorium in good time to see about fifty people standing in groups beside the chapel.

'Hey, Norman,' I said to the superintendent who grows mediocre leeks, 'Is there another funeral due?'

'No,' replied Norman. 'They're all yours!'

'Cor blimey; I'll have to give an address. Do you know anything about the deceased?'

'Just that he was ninety-six and died in hospital. You'd better go up and quiz the mourners.'

I did.

One told me that they were all neighbours. The dead man had worked for fifty years as a carpenter in London.

'Even at his age he was good. Only a month ago he

corrected a table for me which had wobbled for over ten years,' one volunteered.

Another said, 'He was more than a carpenter; he was a cabinet maker.

The cortege arrived. Out of the solitary car stepped the bedfast old lady. Lightly she tripped down the aisle in good steady fashion. She was under five feet tall yet so stately and dignified.

I gave my address.

'What more noble profession could William have followed than that of a carpenter? Jesus was the carpenter of Nazareth!'

Then I went on to eloquently express the virtues of hard woods; run of the grain; true angles; good joints and the ability to recognise suitable woods. I surprised myself at the knowledge that must have come from my sub-conscious for on that subject I am quite wooden and find it difficult to distinguish between solid oak and plywood. Most coffins have deceived me!

'Finally I am sure that the Eternal Carpenter and William have had much in common to talk about. The Book of Revelation assures us that there are trees in heaven!'

The service over, I stood at the back of the chapel to commiserate with the mourners. The dear, old widow came up to me. Tears filled her loving eyes. She looked up into mine and holding my hand as if to comfort me she said, 'Your address has been a great comfort to me; but he wasn't a carpenter; he was a plasterer.'

That plastered me!

I had the opportunity to become plastered four months later. The old lady joined her husband amid the plantations in Heaven. I conducted her funeral. There was only one mourner besides myself; her solicitor. As I was leaving the chapel after the service he said to me, 'The old lady wanted you to have this,' and he handed me a bottle of navy rum.

Shortly afterwards I attended a seminary in County Durham.

'We are told in St Mark's Gospel that Jesus was a carpenter. (Mark, Chapter 6) but was He a carpenter?' asked the lecturer.

I had always thought so and displayed my abyssmal ignorance by stating so.

'Ah,' spoke my informant, who felt quite sure that he had a fall-guy in me, 'the Greek word employed means a workman and not necessarily a carpenter. The best stonemasons were found in Bethlehem just as today the best ship-builders are to be found on Tyneside.

'Hold hard there, Jimmy,' I interrupted, 'I've just come from north of the Border.' I had a fall guy in him. He ignored me of course.

'The Greek word used is *tekton* which means a workman. Stonemasons would travel far and near to ply their skills. *Tekton* could mean a mason or a builder much more than a carpenter. The Arabs use it today to describe a stonemason. The ancient craft flourished in Bethlehem and it is extremely probable that Joseph was a worker in stone who moved to Nazareth to obtain work and stayed there. Most masons of that time worked in both stone and wood. There were no specialists in wood alone.'

Since that faith shaking declaration I have been assured that Jesus did in fact live but was not born on December 25th. Feeding everything known about the time into computers and after three years of research and exploration the computers have now come up with the actual date and even the day of the week. There had been a conjunction in 7 B.C. of Saturn, Jupiter and Pisces. To the ancient astrologers Jupiter denoted a Messiah and Pisces a fish and a fish denoted Israel. Herod, Cyrenius, Augustus, census proclamations and much more accumulated knowledge led the computer to declare that Jesus was born on Tuesday, 15th September 07 B.C.

Topping out

'Census ahead; please stop if requested'. So read the traffic sign and red and white bollards narrowed the channel to a single causeway.

I lowered my car window.

The Amazon blotted out the sunlight. She was straight from a Nazi concentration camp. She was built like a bulwark which seemed to be magnified by the brilliant luminous, yellow overjacket she was wearing and which could have served as a bell tent for a platoon. Her loose, flaxen hair was meant to be seductive but it irritated me as the roots were black.

'Good afternoon,' her voice re-echoed across the fields, startled starlings steered clear and my shock absorbers did a wobble. 'Where did you come from?'

I looked around me. I saw the rolling fields and the distant hills. I lifted up my eyes unto them and contemplated the depths of the azure sky. I heard the sounds of nature and I sighed.

'Where *did* I come from?' I asked myself. Creation and the recreation of Springtime appealed to my innermost soul. The voice of command recalled me.

'Where did you come from, sir?'

'You have just asked me a most profound question. It is a subject that has occupied the minds of philosophers and theologians for centuries,' I replied, 'and can I sum it up thus:

"Where did you come from, baby dear?
Out of everywhere into here!" '

The censor sighed. The sigh was strangled at its birth for her ample bosom was too heavy to heave.

'It's a simple question, sir,' she said, 'where have you

come from?'

'Blagdon,' I capitulated.

'Name of street, please.'

'There are no streets; I live in a farmyard.'

She cackled, she crowed. I thought that she was about to lay an egg.

'You must have an address.'

'Yes; Blagdon.'

She wrote 'Blagdon Village'.

'It isn't a village,' I corrected her.

'What is it, then,' she was getting mad. I was enjoying it.

'Just Blagdon.'

'Very well; now, where are you going?' She was exasperated.

'I would love to know,' I replied.

'Don't you know where you are going?' Her eyes reflected the poison of the gas chambers as she spoke with scorn.

'Well it doesn't matter where as I have friends in both places,' I teased and then I told her of my intended earthly destination. 'To perform a topping-out ceremony.'

'Topping-out?'

She thought better of prolonging her inquisition and said, 'Thank you, sir, you may proceed.'

Before I raised the car window I heard her say in a hoarse whisper to the attendant policeman, 'There's a candidate for the cuckoo's nest.'

The six storied office block stood like a sightless skeleton. Its bones were grey, rough, breeze blocks bonded together with the marrow of crudely applied plaster. The ribs were scaffolding ties and it stood in a grave of lime dust. The floral tributes were discarded cartons from a nearby Chinese take-away. Standing like a disappointed under-taker a uniformed security guard paid silent tribute. The news had just filtered through of the sudden demise of the building contractor.

'Is the topping out ceremony still on?' I asked.

'Yes, sir,' replied the guard quietly so as not to disturb the sanctity of bereavement, 'Just go through that gap.

You'll find the way.'

My steps resounded with sepulchral hollowness and I found my way barred by a high and long tarpaulin sheet strung across the entrance. I could hear voices beyond the Rubicon. How could I reach them? Above the babel of many tongues I raised my pitiful plea; 'Hello there, how can I get in?'

No answer. I searched around for an entrance without success and returned to the impeding tarpaulin. A wheelbarrow with the remnants of hardening cement coating the inside stood nearby. I pushed it against the tarpaulin and clambered into it to peer over the curtain. My eyes just topped it. The barrow wobbled, my feet were setting in the morass of concrete mixture so with a certain understanding but a sense of great instability and imminent disaster I shouted as loudly as I could.

'Hello; how do I get in?'

'Oh, look, everyone, it's Jack.' Cameras flashed. The barrow capsized.

I was led into a transformed ground floor. I was transformed, too, for from the scene of dereliction and debris, like a golden Phoenix spreading warmth and light, there ascended Jayne. Like a guardian angel she took me under her wing and gracefully conveyed me to where there were living fountains of waters or rather wines of varied hues and bouquets. The Good Book promises that they who overcome shall inherit these things so my hopes ran high and came true as Jayne initiated me into the joys of Bacchus, though in the presence of divinity I literally had feet of clay.

A host of business executives were guests. They wore neckties of all colours, stripes, logos, mottos, coats of arms and advertisements, clean shirts and executive suits to match, except for Joe Ging, the Town Crier. He was resplendent in a cocked hat, a pouched jacket suitable for any poacher and silver buckles on his shoes. His legs were encased in scarlet hose which made him look like a 'fliggied spuggy' (a newly flighted sparrow.) His fragile undercarriage was compensated by a stentorian vocal capacity which in turn was supplemented with a long handled handbell. He stood for a while on one foot with his fist inside the bell; Long John Silver!

Joe Ging
couldn't sing;
but they left him about
because he could shout...

'Ladies and gentlemen, pray silence for the Lord Mayor.'

My turn came like the dust cart after the Lord Mayor's show and I wasn't sure what was required of me.

'Don't worry,' said the solicitous and ubiquitous Jayne, 'I'll guide you.'

Workmen wheeled in the barrow that had served me previously as a pedestal. It was now filled with newly mixed concrete. To see and be seen I was elevated to my pulpit; a rickety old chair with Jayne and Joe supporting the back.

'Except the Lord build the house their labour is but lost that build it.'

I began by referring to the collapse of the building firm and the expected collapse of the building and went on to declare that God had asked for his cards a week earlier and then it looked as if the labour had been in vain.

'But I've had a word with Him and He has sent other labourers into the vineyard.' My allegory was appropriate as the bottles of the fruit of the vine stood at the ready.

I gave a short history of the ceremony of topping out.

'The ceremony goes back seven thousand years. A sprig of yew was always placed in or under the last stone. Sacrifice was made, often human. In fact it was the custom to sacrifice the architect for whose spirit was best for the protection of the building but that of its. creator. Our architect is the man over there with the carbuncle and a picture of Prince Charles in his lapel.'

To avoid bloodshed, Bill quickly moved behind a screen of potato crisp cartons.

The area I had to top out was roughly one and a half yards by one yard in dimension. As I smoothed the concrete, so my surplice sleeve gained weight. I stuck the yew sprig in the midst of this conglomeration and then blessed the building.

My speech referred to another building; a public convenience in the Hebrides which, when constructed, was not blessed by the Church but by anxious tourists with low capacity bladders. It was decreed that 'it must not look like a public convenience; it must not advertise its function by displaying graven images of male and female and above all it must not be open on the Sabbath day.' So Sundays became the day when dry walling became wet.

Clerical Canines

'Come here Fifi; shake a paw with the vicar,' called Elaine, the recently bereaved widow. Fifi, with embroidered, tufted coat eyed me with Continental suspicion and looked as if it must be of a different religious persuasion. It remained as stationary as a stone Buddha. Then to display its disdain it lay down!

'*Ici*,' I suggested hopeful for some response.

The poodle came to me and sniffed in a supercilious manner; if one can so sniff, and I was afraid that it was about to initiate me into its tribe by lifting a hind leg instead of offering me a paw. I was relieved to note that it was a bitch! I bent down and stroked it and the *entente cordiale* was established. Then it jumped to my lap and covered my black cassock with dog hairs. I had been told that French poodles do not moult but this one had never read the instruction book or had a parent she did not ought to have had.

'I could not have endured the last ten days without the companionship of Fifi. She has been of more comfort to me than many of my well-meaning friends.' said Elaine, 'Tom's sudden death shattered me and while friends were extremely kind and solicitous it has been Fifi's constant companionship that has kept me from going insane. Have you a dog, vicar?'

'At the moment I haven't and as I'm retiring I don't know if it would be wise to get one.'

After a coffee, chocolate biscuit and a further perusal of photographs I made my way home. As I drove along the country roads I recalled memories of my previous dogs.

Patch was of indeterminate ancestry and was so called as a black patch covered one eye, otherwise he was as white as fuller's earth, when not covered with mother earth from rabbit holes. We had considered calling him Nelson but the patch was over his left eye, or Silver but he was white and had no need of a crutch. Patch was a good watchdog and kept lay-abouts at bay. One such lay-about avoided war service by becoming a full-time air-raid warden. He was a disgrace to that courageous and sacrificing band of guardians.

I was at sea fighting a war.

'I've come to collect your dog!' said the lay-about early in the war.

'Our dog; what for?' asked my mother. My brothers and sister were all away serving in the navy and Patch was my mother's sole companion.

'In the event of an air raid, dogs will go mad so they'll have to be put down now.'

'Patch destroyed? It's my son's dog. He's in the Royal Navy,' protested my mother, referring to me and not the dog.

'Orders is orders,' said the illiterate, dog-hating warden. I only learnt of Patch's demise when I came home on forty-eight hours leave. I couldn't sort out this cruel and arrogant tyrant as he had fallen in the black-out trying to be first into an air raid shelter and lost an eye. Did he trip over a ghost dog? Life has its compensations; I got married!

At the time I was assistant Gunmounting Overseer at the Admiralty attached to Vickers-Armstrong at Crayford, Kent. I had the privilege of lunching with the directors.

'Enoch, you know that rationing and coupons make it difficult to choose a wedding present for you,' said Mr Palmer, the chairman of the directors, but we have managed two gifts which I know you will appreciate. The first is this tea-service and then there's this!' He lifted a very small, black Highland terrier from a box. 'We've called him Bruce. Now he's all yours; the first of what we hope will be a fruitful union!'

Bruce gave us ten years of splendid loyalty. He grew up with the other members of the fruitful union. He learnt to bow his head for prayer and to scrounge biscuits from the Mothers' Union. He saw my transition from naval officer to cleric. He was born on Easter Day and he died on Maunday Thursday.

Why did Mr Palmer call me Enoch?

I had sat at lunch with him and his fellow conspirators when the serving maid annointed my uniform with a generous application of greasy soup. I was loaned a jacket which was much too large, until mine was dry cleaned. For a week I wandered around with the sleeves reaching down towards my knees as if my father had been a gorilla or chimpanzee. The reigning radio comedian at the time was one of a trio, Enoch. The nick-name stuck all the time I was at Crayford.

Bruce had been found dead by my mother beneath an apple tree and lying on a rhubarb leaf. He had been missing all night.

'I've heard that you've lost Bruce,' the dear old parishioner said, 'so I've brought you this!'

'This' was the smallest puppy that I have ever seen. It lay in the palm of her hand. The old, retired schoolteacher, an undiscovered treasure, that is a spinster, was deaf. She had a black retriever bitch which was trained to tell her when the phone rang or the doorbell buzzed. The bitch must have answered the door to a cocker spaniel. In trying to hide its indiscretion the retriever had commenced to eat the evidence. Only Roger survived this cannibalistic calamity. He lived for over seventeen years, suffered a most embarrassing amputation and three different vicarages.

'You were so good to visit me so often when I was in hospital that I really must give you something.'

So said the old gentleman who had been seriously ill but was now on the way to recovery.

'I don't want anything. It was a joy to visit you and in any case I ate all your grapes! I'm just pleased that you are back home again; that is my reward.'

'But I insist,' he insisted.

Not wishing to distress him I acquiesced.

'I want you to have Dainty!'

Dainty was a young bloodhound the size of a camel. She was anything but dainty. Her doleful expression was multiplied in successive folds and wrinkles and her leather lugs accentuated her hang-dog appearance.

Ethel had baked small cakes and scones and had laid them on the kitchen table. We were expecting the Ladies' Working Party. I arrived with Dainty. The angel cakes and currant scones swiftly disappeared into Dainty who in turn disappeared to dispose of the excess burden of her extended stomach upon our best eiderdown.

'That dog goes or I do!' protested a distraught Ethel.

I took a risk. I kept the dog! Ethel and Dainty soon became firm friends. Every day Dainty took Ethel for a gallop but this made them both hungry. I couldn't afford it.

'I envy you your bloodhound,' admitted the Senior medical officer from the psychiatric hospital, 'I've always wanted one.'

'She's yours,' I said but not without misgivings as she had endeared herself to me if not to my pocket. Nevertheless I felt guilty as I watched her soulful features looking at us from the back of a station wagon. Perhaps I was not surprised when I saw her again. She was being returned to me by the doctor.

'I've psycho-analysed her and sadly found her to be quite sub-normal. She's all yours again,' and he hurried away. Only a few days passed when another doctor rang me up.

'I understand that Peter has returned your bloodhound. Would you consider letting me have it?'

He got it, but not for long. He too, returned it. Sub-normal? No!

'I had to bring her back. She brings out the base instincts in my corgi. My dog chases her all over the place. It's just as if a bulldozer had rampaged flattening everything in its wake. There'll be a divorce if you don't take her back.'

A corgi with amorous inclinations towards a bloodhound! Eventually she became a farmer's dog and was well trained and useful. However her exceptional powers of following a scent betrayed her. They led her to rat poison. She died. The corgi died shortly afterwards; perhaps from frustration. I reckon that there must be hell in the dog's Valhalla just now!

It was Palm Sunday. Mac, my small Border collie had survived the restrictions of Lent but was successfully tempted to abandon his abstinence when presented with a mutton bone. He wandered out to the peace of our garden when he heard the church bells calling the faithful to devotions. Guilt stricken he stopped gnawing at the bone and decided to bury it until Easter day. He never recovered it. He had previously arrived home with a wire snare so tight around his back leg that the noose was right in to the bone. Now he had disappeared, never to be seen again. Had he fallen foul of another snare or was there a cowardly, trigger-happy farmer?

This recollection of successive pooches came to an end as I drove into my garage unaware that very soon I would have another dog.

The dairyman's wife sat at my fireside as I returned from Elain's husband's funeral. She had the fragrance of cowslips and silage. Her calf-like eyes were clouded with tears which trickled like buttermilk down her creamy cheeks. She gulped her cud and mooed her distress.

'The dog is going to be put down!'

'I didn't know you had a dog,' I remarked in bewilderment.

'I haven't; I've got a cat.'

'What dog are you talking about, then?'

'The stray that has been about for a week. Surely you've seen it!'

'No.'

'I can't take him because of my cat,' said Sheila, 'Will you? He's so gentle and affectionate. Please Jack!'

So it came about that I entered my yard to find Ethel giving a strange dog a bath.

'I'm using a nettle shampoo.' She informed me, 'He was covered with wood shavings from the Cat and Dog Shelter. Isn't he nice?'

He was, and still is.

What is he? He's ginger with a brindle. The gamekeeper declared that he is a staghound. Billy Clark, dairyman, insisted that he is an Irish wolfhound, but he has never seen one. He was everything from an old English sheepdog to an Egyptian hound until his pedigree was finally established and confirmed by two vets and a dogbreeder. He is a Catalan Sheepdog; olé! We call him Ruff.

One tragic though humorous occurrence stands out in Mac's life. We were on holiday in Scotland. The hotel employed young Roman Catholic theological students as waiters during the summer vacation. Tony served at our table.

'Can you manage to obtain some food for our dog, Tony?' I asked.

'I'll try,' said the young man, 'I'll go and ask the chef.'

The chef was a splendid cook but was stone deaf! He couldn't make out what Tony was asking him. It was no use lip-reading as Tony came from Surrey and the chef from the Orkneys. Finally Tony sank to his knees, held his hands up in supplication and barked. The bark couldn't be heard but the action was understood by the chef and Mac had a good meal which turned into a wake!

'Thank the chef for me,' I requested Tony. He disappeared into the kitchen.

Suddenly there was chaos. We sat wondering what was afoot. Eventually Tony came to us, ashen faced and shaking. He crossed himself.

'The chef has dropped down dead!'

Christine, my daughter is very fond of dogs. She has four labradors. She had a lovely, black, mongrel puppy. It was born with a deformed heart. The vet said that it would never survive. Christine accepted the challenge. All through the winter she nursed it. She knitted it a woollen coat. It responded with a childlike and moving affection but one day her heart gave out. Christine buried it in her garden. She asked me to arrange the provision of a little headstone for it.

'The headstone for Rose is ready, Jack,' reported the sculptor, 'I'll leave it at the crematorium office for you to collect when you are next there.'

When I collected the stone two elderly people were sitting in the superintendents's office. I picked the stone up and walked with it to the door. The elderly man saw the inscription and said, 'Rose; was that the lady's name?'

To which I replied, 'She was no lady; she was a little bitch!'

I meant it sincerely and was nevertheless rebuked for using an expression not expected of a vicar!

Bangers

I was tired as I left the college. I had been marking end-of-term examination papers. I felt despair mingled with amusement! After all the energy and thought I had put into my lectures the answers given in the exams amazed me.

'Charles Darwin discovered monkeys and said that they descended from man'.

'Samuel had been abandoned on a pew in the Temple and grew up to be a twin'.

'Some scholars maintain that the Garden of Eden is a myth but my father saw it during the war'.

'Aristotle discovered that the world was flat while he was in the bath. It is no longer flat as Copernicus found out'.

'William Booth was founder of the Salvation Army and of Alcoholics Anonymous'!

'There are four gospels. Mark wrote one of them. The other writers died before they could copy him'.

Named among the list of Apostles were Abraham, Isaiah, Joseph and even Pontius Pilate! One female student whose mother bred doberman pincher dogs wrote a genealogy of Jesus heading it, 'The pedigree of Jesus'.

The answer I liked best was, 'Bethlehem; the birthplace of Jesus and other kings, e.g. David and Wenceslas'!

I decided to call on my cousin, Joyce.

'Hello Jack, been to the college? Fancy a cup of coffee? I'm just about to put these sausages under the grill. They won't take long. You'll stay and have a bite,' Joyce invited.

Her little poodle, a delightful, friendly dog jumped to my lap and began removing all the microbes from my face with its tongue! My coffee slopped as if hit by a tidal wave. The little dog gained a camouflage coat and my grey trousers achieved a matching chameleon disguise.

'Here, rub them with this,' said Joyce as she offered me a brillo pad. She did the rubbing and almost skinned my leg!

At that moment we heard a terrific crash from outside. In this area of vandalism and graffiti Joyce paid no heed to the noise accepting it as a daily occurrence. In contrast I dashed to the window. Looking through it I saw a car smashed up against a lamp standard. I rushed out. No one else seemed to bother. The driver of the smashed car was a teenager and still conscious. I prised open the offside door and climbed into the vehicle. I yelled for help. The youngster's injuries were severe and there was a great deal of blood about. Skid marks betrayed the fact that he had driven round the sharp corner at an excessive speed and had probably lost control of the car. Someone phoned for the doctor. Quickly a nurse and the doctor arrived on the scene.

The young lad turned his head towards me. He seemed desperately to want to say something. He murmured. I couldn't make out what he was saying. I bent nearer to him as the doctor gave him an injection.

'My name is Keith Woods, I'm sorry...'

He gave a gasp and died. I said a quick prayer.

The police interviewed me, measured the road and eventually had the vehicle towed away. Then a traffic warden hove in sight. He was grey haired and nearing retirement age. He knew the dead youth.

'We'll have to get rid of all this broken glass,' he said, 'Where can I borrow a brush and shovel?'

I was wearing a collar and tie, not clerical garb.

'My cousin will let you have them, I'm sure. Come with me,' I said.

Joyce produced a brush and shovel and the traffic warden got his eye on a second brush.

'You take that one; you can help,' and so we both began sweeping the road.

We had almost finished our task when the warden suddenly stopped and looked carefully at me. I wondered if I was not efficient at road sweeping or if I was brushing against the wind or even obscuring double yellow lines.

'Just a minute,' he said.

'Cor blimey,' I thought, 'he's going to give me a ticket for unlawful parking.'

He walked across to my car and peered inside it. He pondered and had another look at me.

'There's a cassock on the back seat,' he informed me.

'Is there?' I remarked innocently.

'Yes, and now I know who you are! You've no right to be sweeping roads. Give me that brush.'

'Who am I?' I asked in the profound words of the

Psalmist.

'I've seen you on telly! You write books. I've read them all.'

'Obviously then you are a man of good taste!' I congratulated him.

'And further; were you on *Cyclops* during the war?'

'Yes,' I admitted.

'I was the yeoman of signals. I remember you well. Can you remember when we did a moonlight flit from Harwich to avoid the attentions of the German bombers and so frustrated Lord Haw Haw?'

We leaned against our brush shanks as all good labourers should and relived those stirring yet perilous days. We transported ourselves back in time and from the scene of this disaster to that great scene of carnage; the war at sea.

Joyce called us. 'Both of you, stop gassing and come in for a coffee.'

We resumed our reminiscing. Joyce listened intrigued until suddenly she yelled, 'The sausages!'

The bangers were as black as the hobs of hell; mere sticks of charcoal and equally as inedible.

I never got a sausage but now I can park anywhere and unhindered in that little town!

Holidays

'Come ye apart and rest awhile.' Good advice when pulpits, preaching and parishioners became a little arduous. So I emptied the jar in which I kept funeral and headstone fees and decided that with careful budgeting I had enough to allow a short holiday. We had to take Ruff for the only time that he endured kennels he came back with rheumatism. First he had to have his booster injection. That would normally cost money but I had baptised the vet's bairns and I reckoned on a small 'perk'. I knew that he was in the byres. I found him with a bovine foreleg between his. He performed chiropody as he peeled away the accumulated excess of cowhoof. The beast, that is, the cow, turned its baleful optics towards me as I approached with the dog and reacted in such a sudden manner that the vet was almost ruptured. With a gasp and a grunt he recovered by which time the cow had rejoined her sisters.

'Your missus wanting her feet trimmed?' he asked.

'Well, I might send her along if it's free but first I would like you to give Ruff his booster.'

'Aye, come on Ruff, come with me,' and the dog was needled!

I noticed that the cows were wearing yellow, round discs in their ears.

'What are those tallies for in the cows' lugs?' I asked.

'They are fly deterrents. Fancy one in your ear?' I was offered. So it came about that Ruff had his injection and I had a fly disc rivetted to the right side of the brim of my soft hat.

The highland dew which is the equivalent of three days' tropical torrents had kept us indoors for a couple of days, but now the dawn broke clear and bright. A waterlogged spider's web looked inefficient as it sagged on an outer window pane. The nearby trees slowly cried the remaining raindrops from their downturned leaves. A solitary seagull, far from its native environment, squawked its protest at the departing clouds from the chimney top while hardy sparrows deloused themselves in the little puddles which reflected a promising sky

The dog followed the trail of a bitch in season as we crossed the precarious wooden bridge which spanned a river in full spate. Our goal was the antique shop. It sold little that was old but had a good selection of tweeds and an antique lady proprietor. On the counter of the shop stood a bowl of mint sweets; pan-drops in Scotland. I stealthily placed one in my mouth just as the kindly old lady approached me. She was all arsenic and old lace; the old lace was in the tweed and the arsenic in the price.

'Can I help you?' in a voice mellowed and honeyed by antiquity. I tried swiftly to swallow the pan-drop but it stuck like a cork across my throat. I couldn't speak! She looked at me anxiously and her gaze took in the yellow fly deterrent disc in my hat. The light of realisation illuminated her mind.

'Ah!' she fairly shouted, 'I'll come to your good hearing side. Forgive me, I didn't know that you were deaf!' The pan-drop dropped.

It was a short walk from the shop to the hotel. Here was the bitch in season and also my wife's brother, Norman with his wife Jean. They had come to join us in a bar-meal.

In the bar I did not require a hearing aid but had urgent need of an interpreter. The sonsie lass behind the bar spoke fluid and rapid Gaelic as she dispensed the liquid gold of the glens with Caledonian canniness.

The 'Ploughman's lunch' was listed and the 'Crofter's Piece'; Haddock in grease became 'Deep-fried Tayside Turbot' and the speciality, black pudding was served in cylindrical form as 'Legless haggis'!

Perhaps it was the bracing aroma from the bar which inspired Norman.

'Let's go to the distillery along the road.'

'What are we waiting for?' said Jean, 'they dish out free drams!'

We entered the same way as the grain but on foot not in bags. Grain was being smoked over peat. We looked at wash-out tubs and reached the vast vats of copper where the distilling takes place.

Norman was breathing deeply.

'You alright, Norman?' asked his anxious spouse.

'Yes,' he grinned, 'there's a delicious nip in the air,' and resumed his breathing exercises.

This cathedral-like chamber contrasted greatly in my mind with the wooden shed next to a netty; an outside, earth lavatory, which I had seen when attending a wake in the Mountains of Mourne. There they made moonshine which shed sunshine into the gathered mourners.

'We will now go upstairs to the massive water-butts where...SCREAM!' The female guide came to an abrupt halt both physically and vocally. Her Scots kilt wafted as her knees knocked. Before our very eyes an inconsiderate mouse had fallen from the roof above us to land on the step ahead of us.

Norman strode fearlessly and manfully, a modern Galahad, towards the wee beast and lifted it by its tail. Placing it on his palm he diagnosed.

'This mouse is not dead,' he said with the air and confidence of a professional pathologist, 'It's drunk!' and he smelt its breath.

'Drunk, right enough,' was the second opinion, 'but I cannot kill it. I'll just put it into this bin so it can sleep it off.

I'll bet that it has a man-sized headache in the morning.'

There would be more than stupified mice the next morning for the tourists, after learning all the mysteries behind the whisky, really made a good deal out of the hospitality offered by the distillery at the close of our session there.

'I'd like some haggis,' remarked Norman. I expected him to ask for neeps too.

'I know the very butcher,' I offered, 'Ian McDonald; he's a friend of mine. He owns the haggis-hunting rights at Weem so they are bound to be fresh.'

The butcher greeted me warmly having regard to my spending potential. 'Hey, Jack, nice to see you again. Keeping well I hope?'

'Fine thank you but only because I'm avoiding your beef these days. I don't fancy mad-cow disease. Been haggis hunting today?'

'Not hunting; fishing!' he replied.

'Fishing? It's not trout we want, it's haggis.'

'Aye, aa ken that and it's no' troot that aa'm offering ye. It's the most sumptuous flesh you'll ever taste; aquatic haggis!'

The customers began to laugh. Gullible Norman thought that he had had enough that day with drunken mice and aquatic haggis.

'Aye, the first in the line of evolution,' Ian continued. 'Oh, hello Hamish. Is that Jamie ye've got wi' ye?'

Two men had entered the shop; braw laddies and members of the kirk. They returned Ian's greeting with a non-committal nod.

'Come across here; I want to introduce you to Jack,' invited Ian.

They shook my hand and rattled my vertebrae. Sorting out my fingers I wished them well and hoped for the sake of my rib-cage there would be no farewell embraces.

'This is Hamish, our kirk organist and this is Jamie our session clerk,' introduced Ian. Before I could speak Hamish, looking steadfastly at me said, 'I know your double!'

'What,' said Norman, 'is there another like him? God help us!'

'Yes, an exact double; he lives in Alnwick ower the Border and his name is Jack Richardson!'

'Did he live in Stott Street?' I asked.

'Yes, do you know him?'

'He was my cousin.'

'How is he?'

'I'm sorry to have to tell you this, Hamish, but I conducted his funeral service last year.'

'Oh,' exclaimed the kirk organist, 'is he dead?'

After I had been invited to preach sometime at their kirk; in their canniness they never arranged a date, Ian offered, 'Leave the haggis here and go to see the mausoleum which was recently visited by the Queen Mother. It's been all renovated and is a sight to see.'

I didn't much fancy visiting an ancient boneyard on such a lovely, warm day but, hoping for a discount on my purchase, I agreed to go.

'The key hangs in my greenhouse which is next to the kirk which is next to the mausoleum next to the bus stop,' Ian bamboozled me. We got lost!

'Excuse me,' I said to a young lassie exercising her Highland terrier, 'Could you direct us to the mausoleum?'

'Mausoleum? There's no cinema around here. You'll have to go to Aberfeldy for one of them but it's closed down now and is a fun-fair.' said the lass thinking that we were lunatics.

We found the kirk, the mausoleum and eventually the key hanging above ripening tomatoes and an African giant cactus. The visit was well worthwhile and the building pleasant in an unusual way. As we re-entered the butcher's to collect our haggis I noticed a placard which read, DOG BONES AND SOUP FREE. Congruous no doubt for the keeper of the mausoleum key. This last word is never spoken in Scotland but this was intended for unsuspecting Sassenachs. I must point out that the soup was for canine consumption only. *Cave canum.*

Norman and Jean returned to the wigwam they were renting in Perth, the tang of the highlands in their nostrils, the scent of heather in their hair, free alcoholic spirit giving them endurance and aquatic haggis for their supper. They had obtained some soup even though they didn't have a dog. They had troubled dreams all night.

The sun said farewell to another day of our vacation but the twilight lingered. Two young deer grazed almost beneath our window. Two young dears gazed into each other's eyes as the love-bug, together with the midges, bit them but then they disappointed us by wandering outside our view! In the distant but-and-ben a crofter's dear, silhouetted against her window blind, shed her outer garments like a pugilist shadow boxing and then wrestled in Cumbria style with a stubborn whalebone corset. Eventually successful her shadow was dramatically increased, the light went out and our recurring evening entertainment ceased.

So the doings of mice and men were suspended in the sweet embrace of slumber.

On the Air

With a little wangle or a lot of bull one can justify anything! What is a pulpit? I've stood in many so should know but the Oxford Concise dictionary defines 'pulpit' as 'From the Latin *pulpitum* and it is a platform!

So going to the same tome I discovered that a platform is 'a raised surface; thick sole of a shoe; a raised surface alongside a line at a railway station and the declared policy of e.g. a political party or religious society.'

That's where I come in. I have declared, or endeavoured to do so, the policies of Christianity from all kinds of raised platforms; round ones, square ones, awkward ones, octagonal ones. I have preached from an orange box and from a heap of rubble on a bomb site. I have propounded from a sand-dune in the Sahara, from the fo'c'sle and the quarter decks of ships, and in the Mission to Seamen to a congregation of one!

So my broad interpretation of a pulpit can easily include a microphone and a television camera.

I remembered my previous visit to Carlisle. I was to address a meeting of a Cumbria County women's organisation. Jim had been driving me.

'It's a one-way system. We've got to go this way,' said law-abiding Jim.

It was the way of the lost!

'Let's turn back,' I advised as the hills of Cumbria closed in around us and tourist signs welcomed us to the Lake District. We did, and a signpost indicated 'Carlisle...9 miles'.

'We've got a little out of our way,' suggested the optimistic Jim, 'but don't worry, we'll get on course soon.'

The Shepherds' Rest was on the east side of the city. We

had passed it on our way in. Now that we had found it I had to hurriedly find a gents' toilet. My need was acute! We both charged into the large foyer of the hotel and to my relief I spotted the toilets on the far side. They were like a beacon to a distressed mariner. I hastened through the door bearing the outline of a man; then through a second door. I let all anchors down as I went full astern. The gents' toilet was full of women. Desperately I dashed back into the foyer to scrutinise the signs over the doors. My eyes had not deceived me; it was the gents'! Just then a woman emerged; she was convulsed with laughter.

'You should have seen your face,' she cried, 'I've never seen anything like it!'

'And I've never seen a crowd of women in a men's toilet. What is it, an equality stunt?'

The manager appeared and he seemed to be highly amused while my bladder agonised. I appealed to him urgently.

'Follow me,' he invited, 'and you can use the staff toilet.'

Relieved both physically and mentally I asked him to explain.

'There are almost three hundred women here and they have just completed their morning session and before lunch they all seemed to need the toilets. To facilitate a steady flow we authorised them to use both sets of toilets'

Now on my second visit I was lost again, or to be more correct Jim and I were lost again! One-way systems seem to bamboozle him. It appeared that we were heading for the Solway Firth when we were actually looking for the Radio Cumbria studios. I was due to broadcast an interview on my first book after the one o'clock news.

'It's up here somewhere; let's ask,' suggested Jim. 'There's a chap.' We approached a pedestrian.

'Where are the radio studios?' asked Jim. The Hungarian conveyed to us his ignorance of our language and our whereabouts. We saw a man unloading beer kegs.

'Put one in our boot,' I invited, 'Where can we find Radio Cumbria?'

'Oh, you've come past it. Turn round. Go about half a mile and it's on a hill. You can't miss it!'

'Like to bet?' I asked.

Unbelievably we found it. The delightful lady programme presenter met me with obvious relief and I responded with my Carlisle refrain, 'Where's the toilet?'

I broadcast until three o'clock and then sought directions to the Border Television Studios. We got lost!

I arrived at the studio just before four. Jim left me. I don't know if he ever got home!

'The Reverend Richardson; oh, yes, you're on after the six o'clock news,' greeted the receptionist.

'I've got to get the 6.35 to London. Is ther any chance of recording the interview?'

She was lovely but not hopeful. She rang around.

'Sorry sir, the recording team have all gone. Speak to the floor manager when he comes in.'

He came in at 5.30.

'Right; I'll give you an early slot and I'll arrange for a taxi to take you to the station. Just relax; we'll look after you.'

No man is an island. Chernobyl had a nuclear disaster. Its effects reached the pastoral slopes of Cumbria and the Borders. An enraged sheep farmer seeking compensation was given the slot before the commercial break. It was 6.20 before I stepped up to the microphone and before the cameras. Questions were many; time rushed. So did I to the reception area.

'Where's the taxi?'

'Taxi sir?' said the replacement receptionist, 'No one ordered one.'

'I'll miss my train!' I wailed as a cameraman came into the hallway.

'Can you help the Reverend Richardson?' she explained my plight.

'Certainly. I'll take you,' he kindly offered.

His car was reluctant to start. He borrowed another. We ran counter to football fans going to a match against Darlington. We reached the railway station at seven o'clock.

'What time is the next train to London?'

'You're lucky. The 6.35 is running half an hour late. In fact, that's it now. Run!'

The darkening countryside became mysterious as the train rumbled on and the lights of evening shone from small villages and remote farmhouses. The moon rose; so did I.

I found the guard. 'Which direction is the dining car?' I asked.

'There is none, sir. There is a one-day strike of the catering staff.'

'Buffet car?'

'No sir.' My stomach thought that my throat was cut! I was cold and hungry. A draught battered my neck; a draught would have been welcome! We were over an hour late in reaching London.

Faint and weary, famished and frozen, I hailed a taxi.

There was an enraged queue in the reception area of the hotel. The low rumble of my innards added the lost chord to the organ-loud protests being voiced by a clientele which appeared to have come from the four corners of the earth. The hotel had overbooked!

'I rang from New York and have come straight from Heathrow.'

'I booked five weeks ago from Hong Kong.'

'Anyone here speak Russian?'

'The B.B.C. booked my room,' I feebly added my voice to the babel. Even the dread name of such a corporation failed to elecit any positive response from the harrassed night manager. Eventually he disappeared and was so long in returning that I thought that perhaps he had taken a flight to Hong Kong or was pitching wigwams alongside the Serpentine! He must have been waving a wand.

'Gentlemen, I have managed to obtain accommodation for you at various hotels. We will pay your taxi fare!'

I shared a taxi to the Royal Lancaster hotel.

'I'm an explorer,' said my companion, 'What are you?'

'An empty vessel,' I answered with pathos.

The public rooms seemed to be full of Arabs. I found the reception desk. The two girls were most helpful. While one turned to get my room key I asked the other, 'Phew! for the cost of one night here one could almost buy a house in Northumberland. Why is it so expensive?'

'One can see Hyde Park and Buckingham Palace from here!'

'Can I have a rebate?'

'Rebate, sir?'

'Yes; it's black dark outside, impossible to see anything!'

My room was number twenty-five on the fourteenth floor. The speed of the lift distressed my empty stomach. I dragged my weary feet through the luxurious carpeting of the fourteenth corridor when I saw a mirage! Surely the empty void that was my stomach was affecting my mind and conjuring up that which it so urgently desired. Like a lost soul in a lengthening wilderness my whole being cried out for food...and there it was!

Outside a room stood a trolley. On that trolley stood a thermos flask. I unscrewed the top. Coffee! I lifted the silvered cover of the dish; sandwiches!!

I looked to starboard and then to port. It was an empty sea. I whipped the trolley and its precious contents into room twenty-five and eventually returned the empties to where I had found them. I slept with an easy conscience for I remembered that in the Good Book, David, when he was hungry ate the shewbread which was reserved for priests. God bless David for setting such a good example.

In the hospitality room of the broadcasting studios my previous day's pangs of hunger seemed to be but a bad dream. Here there was everything to eat from cornflakes to bacon, from coffee to whisky. Even more charming than the victuals was the inspiring and beautiful company; Libby Purvis, Anna Ford and Elizabeth my hostess. I knew it was going to be a good day!

'My father is a vicar,' began Anna, 'He had a parish in the Lake District. He also had a large, square beard. One day he had the task of scattering ashes among the hills. The wind was contrary. When he returned home mother had to Hoover his beard!'

This reminded me of a similar occurrence. I had to scatter ashes on the Northumbrian moors 'I sucked my finger and held the wet digit up to the weather. Ascertaining, as I thought, the direction of the wind, I commenced scattering. The wind became circular and irregular. Maybe the departed was getting her own back. Afterwards we had tea in a moorland hotel reputed to be haunted by a commuting ghost. I had grit and cucumber sandwiches!'

Spirited Small Talk

'To ensure a comfortable and wetproof fitting ensure that the waistband is fastened colour to corresponding colour.'

I was baby-sitting and the complications of changing a nappy were manifold. There is nothing now as simple as using a safety pin. All is high-tech!

First, the nappy is alleged to be disposable, but how? I searched for instructions in this direction but finally came to the conclusion that if the worst came to the worst I would kick it around the garden until it reached the point of disintegration! Then how does one persuade an over-active bairn from gyrating?

Finally after gaining a perilous stranglehold on the child I managed to place the nappy in its intended position. Now the simple matter of sealing the thing. 'Colour to colour,' there were four differing colours on each waist band. I managed to get blue to blue on the starboard side but short of slicing the infant in two could not match the blue on the other side. I gave up when the child went blue in the face and I reached for the sellotape and completed an effective job. My granddaughter didn't seem to mind! She then preferred a cold sausage to the recommended tin of Heinz baby food but afterwards appeared to be too restless to sleep. So I inflicted my singing voice upon her. A lullaby; that was the answer.

'Keep your feet still Geordie hinney', didn't work so I tried my favourite, 'Sweet and Low'. It wasn't the baby's favourite. Her accompaniment dispelled the tranquillity of the wind of the western sea. So I tried a lullaby that my mother used to sing to me. It was a wonder that I could remember it as I always fell asleep before she finished it. It was guaranteed to soothe the most troubled breast and maybe too to get rid of the wind! 'Go to sleep my little piccaninny' had just begun to leave my parched lips when in came some neighbours.

'Hey, Jack, shut up, don't sing so loudly; someone might hear you.'

'I hope that the baby can,' I replied, 'What's wrong?'

'You would find out if the Race Relations Board heard you singing about piccaninnies; it's taboo!'

'I like the tune,' I protested.

'Then hum it!'

'I've just managed the nappy changing,' I exulted, 'but mind you, it reminded me of the rule of the road at sea and the Highway code.'

'How come?'

'Well, there was a full tide and strong current and a definite one-way system!'

'You realise that you've been playing with that child's life?'

Amazed, I asked how, for by now the baby's face was no longer purple.

'There's dangers today from broken glass in nappies and also from dioxin!'

I laughed and we settled down to talk as the baby slept exhausted.

'Any local news worth hearing?' I asked.

Joan always was up-to-date with the latest scandals. Bob, her husband had a marvellous sense of humour and laughed at anything that was either humorous or tragic.

'Nothing much,' Joan replied, 'Bill Sharp fractured an arm last night when he slipped on leaving the pub but happily the bottle he was carrying remained intact. Apart from that nowt's happened.'

Just then the telephone rang. I answered it.

'That was from the mother of the bride I married last Saturday to inform me that she is now a grandmother!'

'That's a little premature,' laughed Bob.

'At the wedding service I could actually see that the baby had quickened and so could the verger,' I remarked.

111

'How?' asked Joan the gossip.

'The wedding dress was far too tight and before the service in the vestry the verger warned me "Stand well back, Vicar, or you might get a black eye!"'

'Changing the subject I must tell you of an interesting conversation I had at lunch last Thursday in Rothbury. It's a subject that will interest you, Bob, with your spiritualist connections,' I said. 'This is a very interesting story but there's no actual ghost, but an atmosphere and sounds, although I have heard that one or two declare that they have seen the phantom coach.'

'Before you tell us your story let me tell mine,' said Bob. 'That's why we dropped in to see you. We would like your thoughts on the matter.'

'Righto, fire away,' I invited. The baby slumbered.

'You know Dorothy Cairns, she lives in the old coach house at Dinningham. Her husband is an accountant,' began Bob. I knew her.

'Her house is three stories high. Her son Ian, sleeps on the first floor straight opposite the top of the stairs while their eighteen-year-old daughter sleeps above in an attic room.'

I got the picture.

'One night as young Dianne was going to her room she noticed that Ian's bedroom door was open. Out of the side of her eye she thought that she saw the figure of an old lady sitting on Ian's bed. She turned her head fully towards it but whatever it was vanished...'

Bob said, 'I'm not going to carry on with my story until I've had a drink; any in the offing?' I raided the wine rack.

His thirst assuaged, Bob continued. 'This apparition appeared several times but only to the girl and always disappeared when she looked fully at it. She then confided in her parents but not to Ian in case he became scared.

' "Dianne, darling, what you are seeing is your own hair from the side of your eyes. There's no ghost. Have you ever seen anything full view?"

' "No, mother, but I'm not convinced."

'The next evening Dianne approached the door but this time she swept her hair to one side. She saw the woman. She turned fully towards the spectre which didn't vanish or even move. Overcoming her fear Dianne went into the bedroom and actually stood before the ghost. She was middle-aged, quite pretty though very sad in countenance. She turned her head to look at the pillows on the bed and then smiled at Dianne. The whole episode lasted quite a few minutes before the ghost left.'

'You want my thoughts, Bob?' I said, and then reflected. After an interesting discussion we came to the conclusion that the sad ghost must have suffered some disaster, probably a bereavement, in that very room and had not yet come to terms with it.

The baby's mother returned and quickly adjusted the nappy as dampness had rendered the sellotape ineffective. We all had supper before Joan and Bob left for their home.

Tide, time and hedgegrowing never waits for man so I assembled my electric hedge trimmer ready for the fray. It's rather like the painting of the Firth of Forth Railway bridge.

My efforts to correct the undulations of the beech hedge only served to accentuate the irregular rifts.

'You drunk?' remarked Billy Clark as he surveyed my efforts. He was joined by his erstwhile neighbour, Jim Sharp.

'I get seasick looking at that hedge,' Jim remarked, 'reminds me of Blackpool funfair!'

'If you can do any better, here's the cutter. Get cracking,' I rebuked.

'Ne feor,' said Jim, 'I knaa a man whe used one of them electric cutters and he's only got one leg now!'

'Oh, come off it,' I replied, 'There's no danger as long as one is careful.'

There was a brilliant flash. I had cut through the cable!! They laughed. I was shaken.

'Better get Davey Bee to mend it for you; you're lucky to be alive,' said Billy. 'Hey, Jim, we might have had a funeral!'

Davey Bee is our resident electrician; an excellent man as one would expect from an ex-mariner who has created shocks all along the Spanish Main to the Charybdis.

'Righto, Jack,' said Davey, 'but mind you, you're lucky to be alive.'

Was everyone morbid around here?

'I was saved by God and a stout pair of wellies,' I confessed.

Davey repaired the cutter and I decided to no longer tempt God or rely on the worthiness of my wellington boots and so locked the machine out of sight. The hedge remains a futuristic shape.

'You once asked me about our ghost when we lived in Morpeth,' said Davey as we sat over a cup of coffee

'Yes, Davey, I'm especially interested as I know the house you were in and recently visited it. A lawyer now occupies what used to be your living quarters. Strange to say, it was from the window of that very house that I saw a dead donkey! Isn't it funny how many people go through their lives and never see a dead donkey. Have you ever seen one?'

'Definitely not,' replied Davey, 'and I don't think I know anyone who has. How did you come to see it? Was it walking up the road?'

I laughed. 'No, as I walked to the window I watched a lorry pass by. Lying in it, obscured from the ordinary pedestrian, lay a dead donkey. I think that there ought to be a club of persons who have actually seen a dead donkey. It would be unique!'

Davey now took over.

'The house is an old three-storied building. From road level to the top floor there are fifty stairs. I've cursed them many a time when I had to climb them especially when I'd had a night out with the lads. The toilet was downstairs!'

'You must have had an athletic ghost or a very weary one,' I quipped.

'Well, we didn't see any ghost for a long time, neither did

we know of one or expect to have one resident. My young daughter's bedtime approached.

' "Time for bed," her mother said.

' "Can I not stay up for a little while? I'm not sleepy."

' "Bed, young lady; and now!"

'With a backward glance toward the television she reluctantly obeyed her mother. Almost in a flash she was downstairs again.

' "Mummy, there's a woman on the stairs"

' "You're watching too much television," I said to her, "Now, back to bed...or else"

'We thought nothing of this until my daughter woke up one night. The temperature of the room had plummeted. She screamed. When we rushed into her room in response to her cries we felt the chilled atmosphere.'

' "Mummy, there was a woman sitting on the edge of my bed. I'm terrified!"

' "Come and sleep with us; you'll be alright," we offered.

'After a further night or two the ghostly woman returned and my daughter had a good look at her and was no longer afraid. The spirit was smiling and had a benevolent face. So kindly were her features that all fear was removed.

'We lived there for eight years and the phantom female frequently appeared.'

'I know that years ago that house was the workhouse master's residence. The actual workhouse was next door,' I said.

'Yes,' said Davey, 'We found that out too. Evidently the master was allowed to use the younger vagrants as homehelps. There are terrible stories about child abuse occasioned by that villian.'

'What you say is most probable for I too have heard about the infamous workhouse master but I must be very careful as to what I say as some of his descendents still live in the area,' I remarked.

Davey continued, 'His sister was widowed and came to live with him from Yorkshire. She was kindly and did her best to alleviate the lot of the young girls much to the annoyance of her brother. She caught him one day doing dreadful things to a young drudge and she rebuked him severely. From then on she was watchful and protective but he grew aggressive. Finally she is alleged to have fallen down the entire fifty stairs and broke her neck. Many thought that she had been pushed. The master must have had her death on his conscience for he took to drinking heavily and was finally transferred to a lunatic asylum.'

'Very interesting, Davey, but what about my cutter. Is is safe now?' I asked.

'Safer than you are!' he exclaimed.

Posthorn Postscript

'The hearse driver was telling me on the way back from the funeral that one's body can be embalmed for £19.50!' I was relating to Ethel upon my return from a crematorium. 'He reckons it's a bargain buy!'

'How long does the embalming last?' asked Ethel.

'He informs me that it lasts for ever,' I replied.

Then Ethel asked the obvious question, 'How do they know that?'

Well; how? Do they exhume them at intervals?

I decided to keep the embalmers at scalpel length and have a light lunch, after which I remarked, 'I'd better finish off cutting the hedge by hand shears. I'm not risking that electric cutter anymore.'

Soon my arms were tired and the hedge still rather ragged but I was determined to finish the job, as the annual garden competition judging was imminent. Each year a garden seat and a cheque was presented to the owner of the best-kept garden. There used to be a booby prize of a load of cow manure but since the emphasis has moved towards organic farming such treasure as a ripe, stinking load of natural manure is difficult to come by. Last year I should have won that coveted award but instead they were polite and awarded me a plaque for my garden gate which read, 'For great endeavour and faith'. Doubting the real strength of my faith the donor of the prize also gave me a book entitled *How to Cheat at Gardening*. I've put some of its suggestions into practice this year in the hope that the judge has not read the same book.

Like a pruned twig I crept into the house for a refreshing drink. I sat in my chair, bare bust, and wearing green-stained gardening trousers when the doorbell rang.

It was Bob, my neighbour and his wife. They must have heard the rattle of teacups!

'Jack, you never told us that story about Rothbury you were about to embark upon yesterday when we got sidetracked into ghost stories. Care to tell us now. I could just do with a cuppa,' said Bob.

'It begins at Rothbury but moves to the Northumbrian moors. Two weeks ago I was invited to lunch at a friend's home at Rothbury. Her father had served with me at the Missions to Seamen and her grandfather had held the very first master's ticket ever issued; the actual number one. Since her father died Pat has maintained a much valued friendship with us. She knew of my interest in ghost stories and local legends and had invited me with the promise that I would not only hear a ghostly account but meet the persons who had witnessed or heard the uncanny proceedings.

'I sat on a window seat together with another Bob. My eyes, which are really too large for my stomach's sake, had lingered over the sumptuous gateau and I had endured the main course in the hope that I would be the recipient of a large chunk. I was eating my second helping and had a cup of coffee on an occasional table before me. After this disgusting display of gluttony I felt that I must stand up and stretch myself to allow the ingredients of my crowded stomach somehow to subside.

' "What a wonderful view you have here, Pat; it's an artist's delight. Just look at those rolling hills and the changing colours and lights. It's truly romantic."

'Dora sat on the settee opposite to me.

' "Romantic it might look just now but there are dark things out there on the moors, and I don't just mean at night-times."

'Dora has lived her life in the environment of Northumberland's rolling moors. She is a talented poetess and has actually enshrined this story in poetry.'

'Is this going to be a long story, Jack?' asked my neighbour.

'Yes.'

'Then we'll come back this evening to hear it.'

'Suits me,' I replied, 'it will give me a chance to have a bath and get into some comfortable things. See you tonight then.'

Evening came; so did my neighbours.

'I sat enthralled as Dora continued her story.

' "Snaking its tortuous track from across the borders the old coach road followed the ancient paths of Scots reivers and sheep-stealers. For hundreds of years travellers have sighed with relief when the road lay behind them. In all ages it was a Devil's highway; its wheel-ruts stained with human blood and churned by the horses of highwaymen and murderers." '

An uncomfortable thought crossed my mind; my neighbours' ancestors had probably been hanged as miscreants along the borders at one time! However I carried on.

'Dora lives within sight of Rimside Moor, the grim haunt in past centuries of highwaymen and cut-throats. There was a spring on the moor above Gate Burn. There horses would be stopped to allow them to drink of the fresh water while vigilant coachmen and escorts would keep a keen watch. Danger threatened every delay.'

'I know Rimside Moor,' said my neighbour, 'I think that there was a gibbet there at one time.'

'Well, Dora told me that the old road was finally closed in 1850,' I said.

'Yes,' said my listener, 'but one can still see signs of it especially the old crossroads and the ruins of the inn that stood there.'

'Dora had continued, "My husband and I often walked the old road. On our way we would pass the cottage where old Jimmy, the undertaker used to live. You'll be interested to know this, Jack; I saw one of Jimmy's receipts for a funeral. The total bill came to £7!" '

I Mentally compared that cost with the hundreds of pounds required today to bury someone. Even today I know of a few old ladies who have conscientiously put aside £30 or so to pay for their funeral expenses!

' "As we left the village we could see the old coach road;" '

A thread of green across the moor's brown face
a fading remnant left from bygone days.
The old road climbs and spans twin moorland
  streams;
fringed here by stately beech trees
where shafts of sunlight gleams.

' "The old coaching inn at the crossroads is now a skeleton of tumbled stones. At every visit we felt the sinister atmosphere; I would never go there alone. We always gained the impression that we were being watched! Perhaps we were by ghostly denizens from yesteryear." '

Musing by the inn's old walls now crumbling and
decayed
in flight of fancy I am bourne back to the old world
days;
I raise the misty curtain which shrouds forgotten years
and think I see the stage coach with its travellers draw
near.
I hear the post horn's clarion note, the limbering
wheels and hooves;
the folk who dwelt here spring to life; they live and
speak and move.

The 'evergreen' is a mystery! Surrounded by a crumbling wall and the relentless moor of bracken, heather and scrub, there is a large area of green, unspoilt turf. There no weeds flourish. Not a single nettle stings. The sward is pleasant and as well presented as any well-kept lawn. Who keeps it? No one living!

And whence this plot of tender grass? This walled-in
evergreen.
neglected through the ages; yet no weed is ever seen.
Perchance at night while mortals sleep, some ghostly,
mystic power
returns to tend and care for it throughout the
dreaming hours.   .

'Dora continued, "I must give you the complete picture and I do hope that you will go there yourself soon. In bygone days coachmen would prefer to hasten across the moor, resisting the hospitality of the old inn and seeking the safety of The Jockey in our village. It was the custom in days gone by to hang the highwaymen and thieves at the crossroads on the moor and that is where my husband and I had a frightening experience. He was blind. Together, hand in hand, on a lovely summer's day, we wandered on the moor attracted by the evergreen. Walking down the hill towards the old crossroads we heard a sound that froze us to the ground!

' "He turned his sightless eyes to me and said in a tremulous whisper, 'Did you hear that?"

' "Yes."

' "What would you say it was?"

' "Without hesitation I responded, 'it was the post horn.' He agreed. We were too far from any vehicle carrying road, byway or highway. The sound seemed to come, not through the air but from the ground. We never mentioned this episode to anyone until a lady from the village together with her sister rode their horses over the old coach road. As they approached the fresh water stream near to the ruins of the inn their dogs and horses stopped dead in their tracks and refused to move. The dogs growled; the hair on their backs bristled and the horses became nervous and restless. They had no alternative but to turn back and head for home. This they did with some relief as the whole atmosphere had been cold and uncanny!" '

Bob, sitting with me on the window seat, underlined that impression.

'I have been up there on the brightest of days, when the sun was shining, and even settled down to a picnic on evergreen but at all times the atmosphere has been how can I put it, other-worldly and mysterious.'

'Dora continued, "We had picnics there too for despite everything it is a favourite spot of ours, but without fail something would go wrong."

' "How?" I asked.

' "On one occasion I took three of the village children. It was a glorious day without a cloud in the sky. The morning mist which had earlier shrouded the moor had cleared away and we were set for a warm, sunny afternoon. We laid out our picnic near to the ruins of the old inn adjacent to the crossroads where at one time stood the gallows from which many a sightless corpse had swung in the winter winds. At first the atmosphere was wholesome and anything but frightening. The happy bairns kicked off their shoes and took off their socks to play in the stream below the spring. It was all so beautiful and calm."

' "Good," I remarked, "For the children's sakes I am pleased that there was no evil atmosphere."

' "Ah, but there was; it didn't stay like that!" said Dora ominously. "We had just unpacked the food and goodies when quite suddenly a big, black cloud blotted out the sunshine. It was all so unexpected. Huge drops of rain pelted down and we scrambled quickly to save the food and get to some shelter. The only place was under the little bridge which crosses the stream. We huddled under it as the lightning flashed and the thunder rolled and echoed across the moor. A further danger hazarded us; the stream began to flood and we had to find larger stones upon which to stand. It seemed to be ages before the sudden storm stopped just as suddenly as it had begun!"

' "You would be thankful when you got back home," I remarked.

' "Thankful," said Dora, "but mystified. The village had not suffered the storm!"

' "That must have been most unpleasant," said Pat, "you wouldn't venture there again in a hurry."

' "We did," continued Dora, "with my husband and a fellow blind acquaintance. Again it was a glorious day. 'No fear of a storm today' said my friend's wife as she looked across the moor towards the Cheviot hills. We certainly did not have a storm but things were quickly ruined for us. For the occasion I had baked a raspberry pie. We laid the food out on a large cloth and had reached the moment for eating the tart when a loud buzzing made us look up. A swarm of excited wasps descended upon us and swamped the raspberry tart out of sight. This could have been very serious for the two blind men would not have known if a wasp had settled on a slice of tart as they put it to their mouths. I upended the table cloth thereby casting the tart and the wasps away from us and then guided the two blind men to a safe distance before we collected our things and retreated homeward."

' "That could have happened at any place where you

123

exposed a raspberry tart. It was bound to attract wasps!" I remarked.

' "Yes, but it happened there just as on our next visit. Only my husband accompanied me. We loved the place even though it was associated with ghostly legends and we had both heard the posthorn. We knew of the people who had seen the phantom coach in broad daylight although we had never seen it. We rested on the green near to the stream again. Everything seemed so heavenly, far from the madding crowd; in splendid isolation and no wasps or clouds visible. What could harm us? Nothing!"

' "But you're going to tell us that something did," I said to Dora.

' "Yes, indeed," she said, "Remember that my husband was blind. He eased himself backwards resting his hand upon a large, flat stone. It was only by chance that I saw an adder; a very large adder, basking in the sun upon that stone barely an inch from my husband's hand. If he had touched it it would certainly have bitten him. They don't bite unless molested so I quickly pulled his hand away and pulled him to his feet." '

'It all seems to happen there,' said Bob, 'and I don't wonder. Although nothing has happened to us there is still that awful feeling about the place.'

' "The very last time that I went there with my husband we had almost reached the place when we felt a spot or two of rain. We decided not to risk a soaking and turned for home. We had hardly reached the shelter of our own home when the heavens opened and we had a downpour!"

' "Well I think that I had better head for my home now! Thanks Pat for a truly lovely and interesting lunch," I took my leave.

'At home I read Dora's poem and especially liked the lines which recreated the atmosphere of the old, ruined pub.'

*A plump and pretty serving wench brings in a
    steaming pie;*

*she reads a lover's message in the coachman's merry
   eye.*
*He follows her on pretext to help her carry more
but imprisons her in strong, young arms behind the
   pantry door!*
*The ladies smile; their jewelled hands smooth down
   their travelling dresses*
*while blushing maidens coyly glance and pat their
   curling tresses...*
*But the highwayman beneath the trees has greedy eye
   and cruel,*
*what cares he for a damsel's tears; her pleading or her
   sorrow?*
*He'll gallop north of Rimside Moor and rob that
   coach tomorrow!*
*And cantering by the crossroads he laughs without a
   care*
to see an old companion on the gallows hanging there!
I think that aptly sums up her story.

Of course I couldn't wait to visit the moor myself. I
invited Ian to accompany me for he is a biased sceptic!!

'Look Ian,' I said, 'there's the evergreen. Beginning to
believe?'

'Not likely,' he replied as he and I looked over the moor
and saw the fresh green sward standing out like an oasis in
the midst of a desert of brown, autumn bracken.

I began to hurry. I was impatient to reach the spot. It
was just as Dora had described it. There were the tumbled
walls of the old inn, there the spring and the stream and the
little bridge under which she and the children had
sheltered. More so, there was also without a doubt a
coldness on that warm, autumn day; a chill that seemed to
whisper, 'Get away, you've no business here.' To me it was
the kingdom of days gone by and we were trespassing. To
Ian it required more investigation. We traced the buildings
of the old inn, the stables, the courtyard and the crossroads.
All the time I could feel the uncanniness of the place. It
could have been my imagination as Ian suggested, but it

was not my imagination that conjured up the deluge that descended upon us 'out of the blue', literally! We scampered for shelter under the bridge.

'Now, Ian, what about that?'

'Could have happened any day in the autumn!' he replied with justification.

I'm going to return to Rimside Moor again soon, with Dora and Bob!

The 'Bish'

'Request men and defaulters fall in on the quarter deck,' was piped at 11.00 and the hopeful and the fearful duly assembled before the captain's table. I was there not in either of the former categories but in my right as a chaplain, as any man can appeal to the chaplain in confidence for guidance at this reckoning hour.

The master-at-arms is the real power behind these proceedings. To occupy such an elevated rank in the Royal Navy one must come from a single parent family and to be unloved even by one's mother. He stood at one end of the table while the sheep stood on the port side and the goats on the starboard side.

Having no known father the master-at-arms is known as 'The Jonty'.

'Very well, Master, carry on,' ordered the captain.

'Able seaman Higgins, CDX 645371.'

Able seaman Higgins responded to his call by doubling up to the table, saluting and retaining his cap on his head.

'Request permission to grow a set, sir,' barked the Jonty.

A set in the navy is the complete growth of all facial fungus; the moustache and chin whiskers. One must have a reason for this request. The real reason is usually that the ship is leaving its home port and will not be returning for a long period therefore why bother shaving every morning. It's sheer laziness but that is not a recognised reason.

'I have a perpetual sore throat, sir, said Higgins,' and I feel that a beard would act as an insulating muffler!'

'Have you consulted the doctor about your throat?' asked the skipper.

'No, sir.'

'Then report to the sick bay; request put back a month,' was the verdict.

After an epidemic of requests came the offenders. The most common default is that of returning onboard drunk. It is still an unexplained mystery why every drunken sailor on returning to his ship wishes to fight with the canteen manager!

'Ordinary seaman Johnson, sir; did report onboard at 22.30 last night the worse for drink and did cause a commotion in the canteen flat,' accused the Jonty.

'What have you to say for yourself, Johnson? Shut up. Ten days number eleven,' said the captain. All punishments are numbered.

There being no further business the captain turned to me and became a request man himself.

'Bish, can you see me in my cabin right now?'

His request was my command. 'Certainly sir.' (I'm a right creep!)

'Sit down, padre, have a horse's neck.' [that is a brandy and ginger]. Duly supplied he then went on to ask me, 'How's the morale of the ship? Do you really think that it is a happy ship? Is there anything that we ought to be doing?'

That captain was truly a caring skipper with the welfare of his ship's company at heart.

'By the way, on Sunday next shorten your sermon somewhat.'

'Why sir?' I felt a little aggrieved because ten minutes was the length of my normal sermons.

'It's Advent Sunday, Bish, in case it missed your notice.'

'Yes; I know that,' and then the penny dropped. On 'Stir-up Sunday', that is Advent Sunday, Christmas puddings are mixed and stirred on all ships and establishments of the navy.

'Ah, yes, the pudding stirring,' I exclaimed.

So after an appreciated short homilly the ship's company stood by to witness the stirring of the Christmas pudding. Oars are used to stir with and the captain is helped in the stirring by the youngest member of the ship's company. The chaplain has the duty of throwing sixpences into the mixture as it is stirred. I stood by with a bag of sixpences provided by the paymaster who had duly demanded a receipt and the return of the leather cash bag.

We began the ceremony. I began to throw the coins; over two hundred! The Jonty carefully measured the rum into the mixture to shouts of 'throw it in regardless; splice the main brace!'

The amazing thing that particular year was that extremely few sailors found a sixpence in their plateful of pudding and it was thought that the padre was planning an extraordinary run-ashore!

I preached in many ships and to varied congregations in a variety of countries. In Trondheim the pulpit was a three-tier affair and one side of the cathedral was full of N.A.T.O. forces and the other occupied by Norwegians. Being a Geordie both sides understood me! In Lisbon the American Embassy attended St George's Church and demanded the Battle hymn, 'Mine eyes have seen...' None of the hymn books had this hymn; the organist had no music for it so the Americans sang it unaccompanied, quite lustily while our navy hummed! In Beirut Christian Arabs mingled with Muslim Arab dignitaries in the church ashore while I took the service. Happy days then that I wish could speedily return to such a lovely, and at that time, friendly city.

I was with 45 Royal Marine Commandoes in the Libyan desert. The lads were exercising in the Sahara south of Tarhuna. Again they were happy days when King Idris, a personal friend of our Royal family, ruled over a friendly Libya.

I joined the lads when they were resting among the sand dunes in a temperature of over ninety degrees in the shade but there was no shade. I began to give them a 'Padre's hour' and was telling them the most ridiculous Bible stories; improbable tales of the Old Testament but nevertheless true and was having a rip roaring time. Questions were fired at me and I gave lighthearted and improbable answers. It was only when I was finished this most unusual 'Padre's hour' that a man came up to me.

'Padre, I thoroughly enjoyed that; didn't believe a word of it but it was good!'

He was the Brigadier!

On the Darings I used to give a bedtime story over the intercom to tuck them all up for the night but perhaps my most tender memory is that when in *Hood* they played, 'Now is the hour to say goodnight' and that vast, noble and happy ship settled down for the night under the watchful care of those closed up on watch.

Jennie Wren

Old soldiers never die; they only fade away.

Old sailors never die; they are gathered into Davy Jones' locker! What happens to old Wrens?

From my experience of them they grow old gracefully but never lose that stamp that marks the life of seafarers and those in contact with the sea.

They came to me in large numbers for a special service in church; the long, the short and the tall! The round; the rectangular, the lithesome lathes and all with the merry twinkle of mature mermaids in the eyes. Some were dressed like full-rigged schooners while others set the fashion wearing a lateen sail at 45 degrees to their mastlike edifices.

Before they deposited their pieces of eight in the collection plate I preached.

'My text is from Psalm 95 and verse 5; "The sea is His and He made it."

'This planet which we call earth and which as Christians we believe is the creation of God, was it meant for human habitation? I ask this because four fifths of its surface is covered by the sea. Now if God formed the earth to be inhabited there must be a profound significance behind the sea. God formed this earth to be inhabited by making most of it uninhabitable!'

I looked around the congregation from the elevation of the pulpit. Some looked barnacled and natural denizens of the deep. Some I felt sure had webbed feet and scaley skin. Was seaweed the 'in thing' for hair fashion? One or two of the more mature looked well kippered. Others sported cod-like lips and fish eyes but they were all a wonderful bunch. Together they had given several hundreds of years' service to their country. As I looked so memories came flooding back.

'I'm your transport driver; welcome to Liverpool,' so said Olive as she breezed into my office. I had been appointed as Assistant Fitting-out Gun Mounting Overseer and was housed in the Liver Building.

Olive was sparkling; effervescent yet diminutive. I learnt that in the nicest way she was impetuous. She reminded me of my colonel in the Royal Marines who we called 'Spur of the moment Jack'!

'Grab your cap and I'll show you the lay-out of the docks,' and with her handbag slung across her shoulder and her gasmask swinging from the other she didn't wait for my approval but hurried out with me in her wake. She was a true treasure for she knew those docks like the palm of her hand and she also knew all the people who in that seafaring world mattered. Nothing was ever too much trouble for her.

'Good morning, sir; I am your new driver,' said Sheila.

'Why? Where's Olive?' I enquired, 'on leave?'

'No sir, she's in hospital.'

'Sick?'

'No; injured.' Then I got her story.

'Sheila said, 'We call her Violet because when she first came she was so shy and timid.'

'I didn't find her so; indeed the very opposite.'

'Oh yes sir. She blossomed out when she realised that the navy was not going to bully or seduce her! But her nickname stuck in the drivers' pool. Yesterday evening she had been duty driver and was sent to Gladstone Dock. The weather was cold and it was dark.'

'I was down at Gladstone Dock with her yesterday morning. The *Mauretania* had just berthed and I interviewed the gunnery officer. Olive seemed to be alright then. What happened?'

'I don't know the full story but as she was leaving the dock she saw two Dutch sailors fighting. The smaller of the two seemed to be getting the worst of the brawl and Olive swung her headlights towards them. The tussle appeared to be in deadly earnest. She jumped out of the car and dashed towards them, a small slip of a girl, to intervene. In the confusion she was knocked down and her leg was caught under the wheels of one of those large, mobile cranes. She is badly injured.'

'Right; our first journey today is to the hospital. Sheila; pull in here. I'll pop into the shop for some fruit for her.'

'Oranges, sir? They're rationed.'

'They are for an injured Wren who is in hospital. Give me bananas then!' I requested.

'You been to sea for a long time? We ain't got no bananas, straight ones, bent ones, curly ones, we ain't got none,' said the humorous shopgirl, 'but I'll let you have six oranges but tell no one!'

I slunk out of that shop as if I were a felon.

Olive's escapade had not dampened her spirits. She fairly beamed as Sheila and I entered her ward. A large wire cage covered her leg beneath the sheets.

'I'm sorry sir! But you'll find Sheila a better driver than I am. She doesn't go down to the docks at night.'

'What happened?' I asked, but Olive declared with delight, 'Cor, oranges, you been raiding the ships?'

'No,' said Sheila, 'not "rabbits" but genuine, paid for oranges.'

'You're slipping sir,' replied Olive, 'and now to tell you about last night.'

She was the meek, timid little Violet again as she whispered her story which was much as Sheila had related to me. Modestly she regarded what she had done to be just what anyone would have done in those circumstances.

'He was murdering the little guy. I couldn't let that happen!'

Her leg was permanently affected and she came back to the Wrens and served as a receptionist in the sickbay.

I lost touch with her but some thirty years later I was preaching to the Royal Marines on the anniversary of Zeebrugge in Poole, Dorset.

'Isaiah, Chapter 11, Verse 9: The earth shall be full of

the knowledge of the Lord, as the waters cover the sea. The valour and tenacity of those brave men who fulfilled the difficult, hazardous and daring exploit of Zeebrugge successfully, so that the enemy fleet was no longer free to prey upon the lifelines of our nation, serve not only as an inspiration and example, but should flood our hearts with thankfulness.'

Then, as if I needed greater inspiration I saw her! Seated towards the back of the church was Olive. Her hair was grey but her eyes still had that mischievous twinkle and a smile lurked about her mouth. I guessed that she was thinking, 'I wonder if he sees me!' I did. After the service I watched her come towards me as I stood in the porch. Her enthusiasm was uncontainable. She put her arms around me and then surprisingly shed a few tears.

'Sir,' she said, 'Oh sir! I've come from South Wales today just to hear you!'

'Was it worth it?' I asked. 'And please call me Jack.'

'Everybody did behind your back in Liver Buildings.'

She walked with a stiff leg now unable to bend it at all.

'Married?'

'No,' she replied, 'I did get my chances but I got a pension instead!'

The collection of Wrens gathered at the back of the church and I recalled past experiences with them. They all had their stories to tell. I told them of my motley succession of Wren drivers in Liverpool. One was the daughter of the bishop; another danced naked on top of a piano at a sailors' binge and another being a Welsh presbyterian often, I'm afraid, occupied the penitent's stool, or should have done. Yet they were all good girls at heart and the navy would have been impoverished without them.

'I had one driver named Jinx,' I related, 'She was the daughter of a well known soap manufacturer.

'Jinx,' I said as we drove down to Garston Docks, 'What is your real name? It cannot just be Jinx.'

'It is. I've never been christened. When I was born mother was very ill for six months, then I developed pneumonia. My father fell from his horse and broke his collar bone and my aunt when visiting us reached out to take me in her arms and knocked over a genuine ming vase which shattered to pieces. Someone said, that baby is a jinx and that stuck!'

'Well, we cannot allow that to remain like that! What about baptism?' I suggested.

'Perhaps you would like to give me some instructions about it. I really don't see any sense in being baptised for the sake of it. I need to be convinced.'

So it came about that a duchess, countess and a knight stood as godparents for Miss Knight.

'Where are they all now? I'd love to know and to renew our acquaintances; Olive, Rita, Barbara, Sheila and Jinx, sorry, Christine, of course!'

We left the church, spliced the mainbrace and this parish returned to normal.

Suffer Little Children

'Sorry, Jack; tonight's effort is off. My bairn has the chicken pox and I'm advised not to mix in too much company for a while. Might spread the germ and somehow I don't think that you would suit spots. Wouldn't go with your bald pate!' phoned my friend Jim. Tonight's effort was to have been a video film of Jim's new hobby, sailing.

I remembered that there was a talk to be given in another parish on archaeology and the Bible and decided that would make a good substitute for Jim's home movies.

After an interesting load of codswallop by an antique excavator who would have made a good bulldozer executive dealing mainly with pre-historic periods, so pre-historic that it had the atmosphere of myth and fairy tale, tea and archaeological scones were dug up. I'm sure that the scones had a 'sell-by' date chiselled on them. As I do not drink tea and my teeth were blunt I decided to give the refreshments a miss and at the same time be kind to my stomach.

I left the meeting and was walking towards my car when I was confronted by a man wielding a vicious looking, butcher's gully! My first thought was that the authorities were now arming their traffic wardens!

'Is Mr Armstrong still in there?' the knife manipulator demanded.

'I don't know any Mr Armstrong. Who is he?' I asked.

'The chairman of the archaeological society,' was the answer.

'In that case I reckon that he is still in the hall; but what are you doing with that knife?' I timidly enquired.

'I'm going to disembowel the bastard; the b... has had his chips.'

'Steady, man, steady; especially in front of these children. Are they yours?'

'Of course they are mine and I'm left with them,' the knife was fluctuating like a dervish's weapon!

'What's it all about?'

'That b... has had intercourse with my wife. I'll cut him to ribbons,' said the aggrieved father.

'How do you know?' I asked a silly question.

'I dragged it out of my wife. I knew that something was afoot.'

'Where is she now?' I asked.

'Gone,' was the simple answer.

'Gone where?' I persisted.

'To Hell as far as I care.'

'How many children have you?'

'Just these three, thank God,' said the godless would-be assassin.

'Do you love them?' I felt like a Samaritan!

'Of course I do; she mustn't have loved them to walk out on them for another man.'

'If you really love them think before you act.'

'I'm past thinking. He's going to pay for this. How long will they be in coming out?' he asked me.

'I really don't know. What's your name?'

'No business of yours,' was his curt response.

'Right; well it is my business to think about your children even if you won't,' I said sternly, 'You say that you love them. Do you want them to love you?'

'Of course.'

'Do you think that when they grow a little older they will respect a father who is behind bars convicted of murder. Murder it surely is as it is pre-meditated. Give me that knife and go home and think again.'

There was a silence. The long blade of the cruel looking carver was pointed directly towards my innards. I felt unsafe.

'Look,' I continued, 'go quietly home and then tomorrow please consult either a solicitor or the marriage guidance people. They are there to help you. Breathing threats will only get you into deep trouble. Come on, for the sake of the children, give me that knife and take the bairns home. They need you more than ever now.'

Again a pause, then he said, 'Tell that b... adulterer to steer clear of me. You won't always be about. By the way, who are you?'

I told him my identity and promised my help if ever he needed it. Then I returned to the meeting hall to seek out the chairman. He wasn't too pleased with my message!

'Look, leave you car here and let me take you home,' I said as the man protested his innocence.

I heard no more of this matter until recently. The aggrieved aggressor had found solace, not with the Marriage Guidance Council but in the arms of another woman. I wonder if her husband had a carving knife!

I had less success in the next appalling, heart-rending episode which still scars my conscience.

It had been a hard, demanding winter and there seemed to be no let up in the sub-zero temperatures and the cutting wind.

I sat by my study fire. It glowed invitingly as fires often do on frosty evenings. Outside, beyond the closed shutters I could hear the whine of the wind as it skidded over the icebound countryside. I was reluctant to leave such comfort to go to Great Stainton, three miles away up the hill, for a P.C.C. meeting but duty called and I had to go. Little did I know what tragedy was about to begin to unfold.

My windscreen wiper battled gamely against the driving snow and my wheels found difficulty in gripping the frozen snow upon the ground. The hill before me looked formidable. I hoped that I wouldn't be forced to stop until I had passed its summit when at a half way point I saw two figures with outstretched arms obviously hitch-hiking. I continued to the top and then pulled up. Two small girls, aged fourteen, breathlessly came alongside.

'Are you going anywhere near Bishopton?' one of them asked in a Scottish tongue.

'Bishopton? See those lights behind us? that's Bishopton,' I replied.

'No, it isn't. Bishopton is a big town near to Glasgow.'

'Oh, yes; I've heard of the other Bishopton. You're a couple of hundred miles from there.'

They began to cry. The were dressed in thin, cotton dresses without any coats or woollies. They wore no stockings and their shoes were thin and worn.

'Jump in,' I said, 'I'll take you to my home.'

These pitiful young lasses climbed into the back of my car and with great difficulty I managed to turn the vehicle and head for home. Leaving them with Ethel I hurried away to my meeting. Strangely at that meeting it was suggested that the Church make an increased contribution to the C. of E. Children's Society which was once known as the waifs and strays.

Anxious about the girls I risked the frozen hazards of the return journey. I found the girls wearing my sons' pyjamas and sitting in front of a roaring fire. They had been bathed and their flimsy dresses put in the laundry bag.

Slowly and tearfully they told their story. They were 'in care' at a home where the strict discipline seemed to be oppressive and uncaring. They spoke of punishments, tasks beyond endurance, forbidden meals and many other instances which, according to them, amounted to cruelty.

'In the end we couldn't take any more. We escaped through the lavatory window. We hitch-hiked in a lorry. The driver said that he was going to Bishopton. He dropped us about two miles from where you saw us. It was the wrong Bishopton!' said one.

'We're trying to get home. I want my mother,' said the other. 'We would rather die than go back there!'

'Well, I'm afraid that I will have to notify them,' I said.

'Please, please, don't,' they begged in unison.

'Well, I'm not going to turn you out tonight. You go to bed after supper and tuck in nice and warm and try not to worry.'

I rang our village policeman. He was a friendly, understanding man with a young family himself.

'I'll ring headquarters in the morning and contact you and I promise I'll do my best.'

The next morning was a Saturday. The policeman came round in plain clothes; not uniform. He talked in a caring fashion to the little mites.

'You know, vicar, they really do seem to have had a rough time. My heart bled for them as I questioned them. I'm no fool and I know when anyone is trying to pull wool over my eyes but these girls are truthful, I feel sure. Anyway, my superintendent said, that off the record, he will inform the home on Monday, thereby letting them have the weekend with you.'

They enjoyed their weekend but fearful lest they might again abscond I did not tell them until Monday that a car was coming for them. We were heartbroken to see them go. I spoke to the official from the home and informed him that I would most probably seek to get an inspector to visit the place. He didn't seem to care!

We missed them. I rang the home to enquire about them

but the telephonist was quite abrupt. He would not tell me anything about them. I was truly concerned and somehow their tiny, frozen faces seemed to haunt me.

Two weeks later the blow fell.

There was an account of the same girls in the national newspapers. They had been found sheltering behind a hedge on the Scottish borders not too far from Glasgow. The elder girl was dead. She had frozen to death.

'In-as-much as ye do it unto the least of one of these My children ye do it unto Me!'

'Suffer little children to come unto Me.'

She was welcomed in her thin, cotton, frozen frock. God bless her.

Dunkirk

'Late in World War One the British Forces and those of our allies were declared to "have their backs to the wall". Defeat seemed to be a real possibility. God, courage and the conviction that right must in the end prevail reversed the position and the victory was gained.

'Similarly in May 1940 the German forces, bulldozing their destructive and rapid advance towards the English Channel believed that they had trapped our armies against the wall of the sea. Again God, immeasurable courage and a magnificent response to the call to save snatched our men from the very jaws of the mad dog of Europe.

'Many regard the epic of Dunkirk as a miracle. In my eyes it certainly was. There was a placid calm over the sea which lasted most of the period of evacuation and at times a concealing mist. Ships and boats and other craft of all shapes and sizes, seaworthy and unseaworthy defied the enemy and carved into the annals of our history one of its most glorious hours which really marked the beginning of the ultimate defeat of the dark and threatening power of the aggressor.

'The heroism and sacrifices of that time involved great and spontaneous endeavour, unbelievable sacrifice and determined resolve but it exacted a price of death, mutilation and suffering. Today we remember with heart-felt thanks all those who were at Dunkirk, the rescued and the rescuers; the veterans gathered with us today and around similar cenotaphs and we glorify God for His saving activity in those days when we needed it most urgently.'

So I preached, but the most moving and inspiring sermons that day were preached unobtrusively by the veterans themselves.

Before my address I had stood a relatively isolated figure in the large, city square. Although I felt a long way from my fellow men, about four hundred people had gathered behind barriers about three hundred yards away. Astern of me was the massive figure of St George with his sword poised perilously near the dragon's head. Further to the rear two naval ratings stood at the foot of a huge flagpole ready to unfurl the Union Flag. My pulpit was to be the lower step of the war memorial and my immediate companion was a massive microphone.

Over the roof tops and down the wide thoroughfares came the faint beat of drums. This crescendoed as the band of the Green Howards drew nearer.

'Hearts of oak are our men'; 'Rule Britannia' and 'All the nice girls love a sailor', reminded us that this service had a note of thanksgiving to the men of the sea who in all kinds of craft had answered the call to save our beleaguered expeditionary force as well as praise and thanksgiving to God for the miraculous deliverance at Dunkirk.

'Right turn!' the Company Sergeant Major yelled.

A battalion of regular soldiers dressed in the uniforms of the last war and carrying out-dated weapons swung into the square. They were followed by a procession of vehicles which had actually been used in the war. They may be obsolete but they stirred many poignant memories. After

141

the band the dignified, robed figure of the Lord Mayor with his mace bearer together with the chiefs of the three services made their entrance.

'Steady lads; show them how to do it!' ordered the Parade Commander as three hundred and fifty Dunkirk veterans marched into the square.

It was at once inspiring yet heartbreaking to see them. Their very bearing was a silent but eloquent sermon. In smart formation they came; heads erect, shoulders well back, medals gleaming and shoes shining. There wasn't one under seventy years old. They looked at me as I had looked on them so many years ago. Many now wore what scanty remnants of uniform they had treasured throughout the intervening years and many wore the permanent scars of conflict which they had carried since those terrible times of war. A blind man was guided by one with a single arm. False legs were evident swinging awkwardly as their wearers valiantly endeavoured to maintain step with their comrades. Courage; loyalty; pride of country and regiment, determination and sheer guts lightened the lines of age and suffering which their past experiences had etched upon their features. I was proud of them!

The 'Last Post' sounded.

Silently as the flags and banners were lowered we all relived that dramatic and fateful episode when so many of their comrades 'never made it'. They remembered the unrelenting attacks of an implacable foe and the unspeakable hazards of survival. Many an eye was dimmed. I saw the hymn in action; 'Sorrow and love flowed mingled down'.

'Eternal Father' swelled like a heaving sea. They stood erect and immovable, albeit that some were aided by sticks, for the National Anthem.

God bless them all.

I moved among them at the reception which followed.

'What ship brought you off?' I asked.

'I couldn't tell you. It was a destroyer. She was alongside the mole. The enemy aircraft singled her out as a special target but her captain refused to sail until the ship was fully and even over-loaded. I saw it and joined the desperate rush to get onboard. We ignored the firing from the aircraft. I jumped onboard and dashed immediately below instinctively. I stayed there until the engines were stopped safely in Britain again.'

'And what about you? Who saved you?'

'No one. I was with the navy. We couldn't get alongside or very near to the beach. We sent in boats to ferry the lads. I saw a soldier up to the neck in water supporting his mate. I reached over the gunwale to assist him inboard. I took the lad's arm to heave him up and his arm came off in my hand!'

'I was wounded and weak from loss of blood,' said another veteran, 'and came over faint before I could reach any vessel. I sank below the shallow waters but had given up hope, when a sturdy arm took my weight and lifted me bodily from the engulfing water into a boat. The saving arm was that of my own brother; a navy man.'

'That's the Black Watch badge you are wearing. What about you?' I asked.

'What I would call a rowing boat with a single sail had come right up to the beach. Its crew of two were rag-taggle foyboatmen. To me they were sent from Heaven itself. It was ferrying out to larger ships. As we waded towards it through very shallow water a German fighter plane dived at us and I got one in the stomach. I felt the searing pain then nothing. Before I passed out I heard my mate say "I'll get you home, Jock!" He did. I regained consciousness in a Kentish hospital.'

'You had a good mate then, Jock,' I remarked.

'Yes, but he had been wounded at the same time as I had been. I didn't know until he visited me in hospital with an empty sleeve!'

Further stories were told to me; of small craft capsizing as desperate soldiers sought to board them; of the repeated journeys of *The Medway Queen* by one of its crew who stated that they made seven journeys across the Channel

until they could do no more; of soldiers sacrificing their own hope of rescue in order to ensure safety for the wounded and of the untiring efforts of seafarers. They were all given in a spirit of humility and thankful recollection.

'Padre, I like a preacher with thunder and guts! Will you take my funeral?'

So asked one of the veterans as he munched once again at a bully-beef sandwich.

'Well, I've got an evening service to conduct tonight; can you hang on?' I bantered, 'Better still we'd better wait until you're dead.'

144

'I mean it, padre!'

'If I'm still about then I certainly will.'

'You'll be about; I'm over eighty.'

'And what about mine?'

'And mine?'

'And mine?'

'If I'm going to take orders for funerals how many of you would like to pay me in advance!' I laughed.

Men this country must be proud of; today is in their debt!

> 'Unite us in the sacred love
> of knowledge, truth and Thee;
> and let our hills and valleys shout
> the songs of liberty!'

Seeking the Lord

The vice-principal, Long Tom to irreverent students, sprinkled a generous soaking of Worcester sauce over his porridge. Quoting a Hebrew charm-word from the Book of Proverbs, the Old Testament scholar vigorously stirred the sauce into the cereal until it resembled a revolting plateful of ready-mix. Then he pieced his toast into this pottage and remarked;

'Never bother with bacon and eggs myself. This is the stuff to put hairs on one's chest!' yet when stripped to the waist there wasn't a sign of hairy growth about his upper anatomy.

'Jock, restrict yourself to porridge this morning. We've got the cross-country run today.'

'Who else is going?' I asked the V.P.

'Just you and me,' he replied, 'Yours was the only name on the list.'

He swilled the brown cement around his mouth with obvious glee and evil intent!

Long Tom was 6 feet 3 inches tall in his stockinged feet and he had on the very first day of my first term at college affixed a notice to the board requesting volunteers for a cross country run. I put my name down at 6.30 p.m. The notice disappeared at 6.40 p.m.

'It's the first time that anyone has volunteered in years. He tries it every term. When he saw your name he whipped the notice down in case you might learn the truth and cancel it. We should have warned you!' advised veteran scholars.

'Why? What's wrong with a cross country run? How far do we go?' I asked.

'It's not how far; it's how long!'

'How come?'

'He begins reciting the Book of Psalms when you set off and you don't return until he's completed all one hundred and fifty psalms!'

I didn't believe them.

It was true!

'Blessed is the man who hath not walked,' he began. I thought that the more blessed were those of worldly wisdom who were now relaxing upon their beds or cavorting on the sports field. I persevered but faltered often to lag behind to be urged to put forward more effort by the V.P. whose stride was seven feet.

'Be thou my judge, O lord, for I have run innocently,' I retorted from the 26th psalm, 'my foot standeth right!'

I kept up with him with desperate determination and as we reached the 150th psalm the V.P. with plenty of breath to spare said 'Let everything that hath breath praise the Lord.' I couldn't; I was no longer in the category of the breathing.

'Let's sprint for home!' and he set off jet propelled. I flung myself on my bed.

'Turn again then unto thy rest, O my soul,' and spent the rest of the weekend smelling of embrocation and walking

with a zimmer!

College was rather like ship. The principal was an excellent skipper. Many of his students had served in the war. To enable me to carry on my connection with the Royal Navy I had joined the reserves and was listed as Lieutenant Commander (E) R.N.V.S.R. the 'S' standing for Special!

We were allowed 'shore-leave' at weekends only but had to be back in college by ten o'clock. I was returning from Liverpool one Sunday evening in the summer term about nine o'clock. I had to walk past a bomb site surrounded by derelict buildings now used as a 'speakers' corner'.

'No one believes in the virgin birth today,' ranted a free thinking, rationalist orator, 'Only a fool or an imbecile would swallow such utter bilge. Even old ladies smile at the idea today. The clergy certainly don't believe in it but are afraid of preaching the truth.'

Coincidently we had just finished studying and discussing that very subject that week and my mind was full of certainties, platitudes and examples. I lingered to listen to the hairy man on the box. He had beetling brows and from the manner in which he jumped about on his dais I think he also had tape worms.

Slogans bedecked his platform; 'The Church is afraid of the truth'; 'Think, think, think for yourselves'; 'Are you sheep?', and 'You want the truth, we give it to you!'

'Rubbish!' I arrogantly mused as I prepared to walk on.

'Is there anyone here who believes in the virgin birth? It's primitive rubbish for the superstitious and unenlightened; the ignorant and the foolish sentimentals. I challenge any one to declare their belief in this improbable, no, impossible, doctrine. Week after week, month after month, yes and year after year I have thrown out this challenge and have yet to find one single person who believes.'

My big mouth got me into trouble, theological trouble. My voice was as determined as his.

'I believe!'

It was as if he had been struck by lightning. He searched the small crowd with his eyes, disbelieving his ears, then finding his voice and his index finger, stretched his arm towards me and began his derision.

'Look at him, ladies and gentlemen. Look at him. Did his mother never tell him the facts of life? Run away, little man, and study the bees!'

Stung into action I buzzed up to his box-like dais and climbed aboard. I began to address the crowd which now began to increase.

'Get off this box,' raged the tub-thumper, 'It's my meeting, not yours!'

'Did your mother not teach you manners or did she abandon you at birth?' I was naughty but bold.

I carried on. He sought to deny everything I said. It was a 'battle royal' and the combat only ceased when this hairy ape left his platform and sent his aggressive friends to reclaim it.

It was eleven o'clock when I reached college. Late offenders were required to enter the door that led to retribution and correction; the door to the principal's lodge.

'I'm surprised you are late, Jock. What's the excuse?'

I was Jock to both principal and students. I felt very righteous and confident.

'No excuse, principal. A reason, yes,' I answered.

I gave him a blow by blow account of the verbal exchange with Karl Marx and when I finished he began.

'Now what you should have said is this...'

At two o'clock in the morning, not sure whether I had been congratulated or chastised I was released. I hoped that there would be a question on the virgin birth on the exam papers. There wasn't.

The principal was a brilliant theologian and a saintly man with hooded eyelids. He was 'ashore' one day when he was accosted by a man wearing a pyjama jacket and striped shorts. He held a placard warning all and sundry to prepare for approaching doom. In a solemn, sepulchral voice he demanded of the principal, who was wearing a collar and tie, 'Have you found the Lord?'

'Dear me,' replied the principal, 'I didn't know He was lost!'

Seaworthy

It was 'Sea Sunday'. I was preaching in the ancient church of a small, coastal town. From the tower of the church one could view the sea. From the timbered roof, which resembled an inverted boat, hung a model schooner in full rig. Carved saints supporting the pulpit had their feet entangled among wooden ropes and halyards and a stained glass anchor depicted 'Faith'. It might have been faith that brought Old Barnacle to church but it is more likely to have been hope and charity; the hope of being on the receiving end of a shipowner's bequest! His real name was Douglas. He was clinker-built and well-weathered with many a bottle broken across his bows! His legitimate wife had scuttled their marriage years ago. His latest paramour sat next to him in what to her were alien surroundings. She looked like a painted figure-head; breasts that would break any waves and a long nose which would have fashioned a sturdy bowsprit.

The mayor sat in front of her, dignified and somewhat restrained by the willowy mayoress who could have been more plenteously endowed with superstructure. She kept a wary eye on the mayor to prevent him from getting an eyeful of Barnacle's buxom bo'sun.

The harbour master, having sobered up from the previous evening's visit to a frigate, read the lesson from the Book of Acts, chapter 27 with so much gusto that we began to feel the ship rocking. In due season I climbed into the crow's nest; the pulpit. I took a hefty gulp at the glass of water placed in the pulpit to find that some well-intentioned and no doubt nautical person had laced the water with navy rum. What a sermon!

I began biblically. Taking the congregation in thought to the Sea of Galilee I contrasted its peaceful sleeping under the blue Syrian sky with the violent storms that could quite suddenly whip it up into a fury of chaos. 'Save Lord, we perish!'

Then to the North Sea beneath whose depths lies a million secrets and a lucrative oil field.

'As Britons,' I began. I was preaching near to the Scottish border to a congregation which included presbyterians; 'we have the sea in our blood. Our heritage is of the sea. Most of us in this church have family or friends serving at sea. Some personal traditions go back several centuries.'

I began to warm up; to get my sea-legs; full steam ahead!

'Have you ever thought of the heroic daring of the earliest navigators who left our northern coasts to venture into the unknown. What terrors awaited them they knew not. Superstition placed monsters and evil spirits about their sea course. There were no charts for them; no bell on sunken reef; no lighthouse. There was a time when no mariner knew, driving before the wind and facing tumultuous seas, if he was making for the Faroes or the vast wastes of the Atlantic!'

I hoped that I was getting my geography right.

'Yet, in my mind's eye, I see their tiny, fragile vessels faring forth into a world of waters leaving behind them the calm and peace of home and not knowing when, or if, they would ever return.'

Then as a sop to my presbyterian brethren I quoted, 'As Doctor Morrison, the great Scottish divine and learned preacher, so aptly wrote, "Sweet to mortal is the summer sunshine, sweet is the languous shimmering on the vine; sweet is the laughter of children and the crooning of the mother in the home".

'All this was sacrificed by those early mariners as they said farewell to their loved ones and sailed into an alien element that behaved like a wayward mistress.'

The following Saturday there was a street collection in that same town in aid of the Mission to Seamen. I stood in the doorway of a fashionable shop rattling a collection tin. The weather was atrocious. A biting wind sweeping in from the North Sea cut through our summer clothes making them and the season a mockery. Greater mockery was on the way; abysmal hypocrisy!

One woman, dressed well-prepared for the wintry onslaught on that July day was helped from her Rolls Royce by her uniformed chauffeur. She gathered her fur coat about her and was hurrying into the well-lit shop when I stood in front of her.

'Would you care to contribute a little towards the work of the Mission to Seamen. This is particularly for the Shields mission. We care for sailors in Berwick, Amble, Blyth and the Tyne...' I shook my tin invitingly.

'Oh, hello,' she responded, 'Weren't you the preacher in

our church last Sunday?'

'Yes.'

'I thought that your sermon was splendid; quite to the point. We tend to forget the needs of our sailors in peace time. I remember during the war how the church had a knitting party to make comforts for the sailors.'

I could remember them too; I was the recipient of a sweater knitted by a church working party. It was so big that it reached my knees yet the sleeves barely reached my elbows.

'We owe them a great debt. They protected and sustained us through those difficult days. My housemaid lost her husband at sea; torpedoed. I know that even today they endure hardships. We must do what we can for them. By the way, I did enjoy your sermon!'

She opened her purse. It was literally bulging with banknotes. She closed it. Then she fished around the deep pocket of her fur coat and produced one penny which she deposited in my tin saying, 'Every little helps and it all adds up.'

Disheartened I decided to call it a day and drove to the sea front. The wind was lashing the contrary tide into a vast corral of white horses. I sat within the shelter of my car and scanning the moving seascape remembered when I so often viewed the same turbulent scene from ships being mercilessly assailed by unfriendly seas.

Every little helps, so it does but how much is 'little'?

I recollected the time when *Cyclops* and the third submarine flotilla sailed past this very coast. Being warned of an intended air raid upon our submarines in the River Stour at Harwich we had hurriedly left that port for Rosyth. *Cyclops* could only make six knots. A heavy, wet mist obscured our passage. A minefield stretching from John o'Groats to Dover lay to our seaward and it was still in the days when radar was not yet fitted to our ships. At times we felt grating along our hull. Was it mines? Grey shapes ominously appeared out of the fog; shapes that could have been a remorseless enemy ready to destroy but thankfully weren't. Nevertheless our guns' crews were at permanent station with nervous fingers! We were in perilous waters.

'Jack,' said Captain Ruck-Keen, 'keep an open line to your Boss; we need your prayers.'

Our prayers were answered. We reached Rosyth, but sadly as the great conflict continued I lost many a good friend protecting our sea lanes and island.

'One penny; it all adds up!'

I well remember an early January night in the sixties.

The mission chaplain was away and I was standing in. The storm began on New Year's Day. It increased in ferocity as those short days passed in gloom and tempest.

On the third night the driving wind made it hazardous to even walk outside. We couldn't battle against it and if we went in its direction we were blown well ahead of course.

The rocket gave its brief light as it fell foul of the unrelenting blasts. Another rocket screamed its distress call into a combatting sky to extinguish itself upon the Middens off the Tyne. Rudderless and helpless a Greek ship was being driven to its fate on the rocks which were soon to tear its bottom out. The massive waves hastened its demise as it foundered upon the impeding sand and rock. The soul of that ship agonized as it broke its back and the wind screamed a requiem as a thousand demons seemed to hurl themselves against mariner and vessel.

The mission sprung into action and prepared to receive survivors. Joining the male staff I rushed to the beach. Volunteers, in answer to the rockets were already there. Coastguards were efficiently giving orders. We all put our backs into whatever task they gave us.

A lifeline was fired which snaked its way towards the stricken vessel. The gale prevented it from reaching its intended destination. The third attempt was successful. The sailors made it fast inboard. Hurriedly, yet carefully, a breeches buoy was rigged up and we began the task of bringing the crew to safety. The line was too slack but still serviceable so that when we dragged the sailors ashore they had been pulled through the raging surf and were half drowned when they, exhausted, reached us.

Eventually all had been rescued save two. The chief engineer and the captain were still onboard.

'Get ready to heave; the engineer is climbing into the buoy. When I say "heave" you know what to do, and do it with all your might...No...belay that. Hold fast. What's he doing?' asked the coastguard.

'Seems to have gone below,' someone said.

We peered anxiously through the flying spray. The density of the night made it extremely difficult to discern anything. The coastguards had night binoculars. Eventually the line tautened and we began to heave. Through

the raging tumult we dragged the chief engineer. He lay exhausted on the hard shingle for a while then, gathering strength he stood up and unzipped his anorak.

From the shelter of inside he took a wet and shivering puppy. When about to climb into the safety of the breeches buoy he had remembered the wee pup and had risked his life to go below to save it. By then the ship had well and truly foundered and become a total and dangerous wreck. Almost spontaneously three cheers broke out for the engineer; defiant cheers that seemed to rebuke the wind and the waves.

'Every little helps; it all adds up!'

As an epilogue to this moving story of the rescued dog, officials came to the mission the following day. They demanded that the pup be put back on board the remains of the ship which was still being pounded by heavy seas.

'This animal has to be returned to the ship as it has been illegally landed in contravention of the rabies regulations!'

This was ridiculous as the ship had sailed from Middlesbrough and it was in that port that a friendly family had given the ship the pet. In effect it had never been out of this country and not even outside the three miles limit. The officials argued that a Greek ship was a foreign country. The discussions, or rather arguments at some times rather heated, lasted for two days and resulted in the pup being placed into my care on the condition that it did not leave the mission buildings. I bought a plastic tree for the flat roof!

. One sad note. The captain had lingered onboard so long that ten days later he died, with us, of pneumonia.

I recalled all this as I sat in my car viewing the sea. I remembered many more hardships as I journeyed home. No doubt the generous lady was warm in her imported fur coat and well fed with her sea-borne victuals!

Resting in Loch Restil

'I think that you ought to let the doctor give you the once over. You look gaunt,' said Ethel my wife.

Following hard on the harvest festival we had held the November fayre and every week during that period had held several functions in order to raise money to replace the worm-eaten pews and the pulpit which suffered after a weekly dose of dry rot! I was worn out and knowing that the exacting time of Christmas was almost upon us I felt that Ethel's advice was good.

'Get stripped off and let's have a look at you,' said the doctor. I stood before him in the bare magnificence of my manhood, corrugated ribs, arched back, spindley legs and knocking knees. He gazed at me amazed. I assured him that I was human!

'You too could have a body like mine,' I assured the doctor.

'Aye; if I don't watch out!' he laughed, 'Let's see if you have a heart.'

He probed around moving his ice cold stethoscope about my manly chest. Goose pimples impeded the smooth passage of that instrument and when he asked me to cough I almost blew him out of the surgery.

'Talking about hearts, doc,' I began, 'when I was in the navy...'

'Oh dear; here we go again,' said the doctor who had served with the Army Medical Corps, 'let's have it!'

'Well,' I resumed, 'there was a Wren whose entire anatomy was in reverse. She was the wrong way round. Kidneys on the wrong side; appendix appended to the opposite side and her heart inclined towards the right rather than to the left.'

'How did you know?' asked the suspicious quack.

Passing that over I continued, 'We also had an artificer who served under me when I was an engineer who knew everything there was to know about horse racing. He knew the colour of the horses' eyes, what size shoes they took, the height and weights of jockeys and the christian names of stable girls. As a division we had to submit to the regular chest screening. If we heard nothing after twenty-four hours we knew that all was well. Poor old Burchett, the artificer, was recalled to the doctor.

' "Guess I've got galloping consumption," he remarked, "Anyone willing to bet that's why I'm wanted? Give anyone three to one!" He returned from the sick bay laughing his head off.

' "Guess what," he exclaimed, "they wanted another look at my heart. The doctor said it was as large as a horse's heart!" '

'Well, yours is playing up a bit and I wouldn't take any bets on you,' the doctor cheered me. 'You must take a break before the Christmas services. If not you'll not be feasting your face on Christmas goodies. Get away for a couple of weeks. You've still got time.'

So it was that I journeyed by train and bus to the Highlands. When I alighted from the train at Queen Street, Glasgow, the sky had darkened into an ominous grey. A few stray snowflakes dusted the windscreen of the taxi. I was an hour early for the bus so had a warming cup of Bovril at the bus station. The café was draughty and I was, to put it in Northumbrian vernacular, 'fair nithered'. The snow began to fall more heavily.

'It's warmer in the bus. Anyone wishing to board now may do so.'

I managed to get the seat immediately behind the driver's position. The snowstorm deteriorated into a raging blizzard. The streets of Glasgow were covered so deeply that even the traffic could not diminish it.

'We can't set off in this lot,' said the driver. 'Better wait to see if it improves.'

We sat for an hour stationary. This gave me time to study my fellow passengers. Immediately opposite to me across the gangway were an elderly couple well wrapped up against the winter's weather and equipped with a flask, presumably of hot beverage. A young girl sat behind them. I envied her ear muffs which as puffs of mink shielded her hearing appendices while my lugs slowly turned into icicles. Four old highlanders from Campbeltown were wrapped in plaids and bonnets while in contrast three so-called 'Teddy-boys' with bootlace ties, braided jackets, pipestem trousers and platform boots sat behind me. The bus was not filled to capacity.'

'Och, de ye no' think that it's time we were moving?' grumbled one of the Scots.

'It's still rather dicey,' remarked the driver, 'I'll consult the office.'

We thought that he had gone away for a high tea as another half hour passed by without any progress.

'Aye, we can risk it,' he said on his eventual return and the bus began an eventful journey. Looking back I likened myself to Jonah. Progress was slow and hazardous and the first prolonged stop was on Loch Lomondside. An ambulance carrying an injured man from the scene of an accident to the Vale of Leven hospital skidded into the blade of a snowplough. The blade sliced into the side of the ambulance killing the patient and blocking the road. We sat there for an hour and a half. Darkness was intense and the continuing blizzard restricted visibility to a few yards.

'You can carry on now but I suggest you stop at Luss. The road ahead is treacherous,' advised a policeman.

'No way,' said the contingent from Campbeltown, 'Just keep on going. We've got to get there tonight.'

I was pleased when we reached Arrochar for a scheduled stop.

'Right oh,' said the driver, 'All off. We have half an hour here.'

The hotel lounge was full of stranded passengers from other vehicles.

'Ye'll no' mak' it tonight,' said one Jeremiah, 'We've just come down the Rest and be Thankful and nothing is going up.'

I sat by the fire. I had ordered hot drinking chocolate. The old men were drinking wee drams that were not so wee. The Teddy Boys rather unexpectedly were satisfied with straight tea. After two hours and a bundle of grumbles from the old men the hotel served hot soup. While we were guzzling this a policeman came in.

'Afraid you're all here for the night. The Rest is closed. Traffic is stranded at the top. There's no way through!'

Immediately the Campbeltown clan complained clearly and collectively.

'We say we carry on. We ken this road; we'll get

through.'

'I shouldn't advise it,' insisted the policeman.

'We got on this bus at Glasgow to go to Campbeltown tonight, not tomorrow,' grumbled the Scots, 'Let's awa' the noo and ne dilly dallying.'

'We're quite happy here for the night,' chorussed the Teddy Boys with their wandering eyes on the tartan clad serving girls who were responding favourably; 'anyway it's not safe to go on.'

'What de ye ken aboot it, laddies. We were born and bred aroond here and I reckon we know the weather and the bad spots. Ask yon lorry driver; he's regular up here. The wind winna' blaw his lorry into the loch!'

The lorry driver and his mate came across to us and were joined by our driver. They finally decided that it was improbable that the wind could seriously affect a huge lorry laden with massive tree trunks.

'Follow me closely, Keep on my tail and you should be O.K.' suggested the lorry driver.

So we piled into the bus again and set off. Things went alright until we reached the bottom of The Rest. Then we found it difficult to grip the windswept frozen road. Snow was still blanketing everything out and was freezing as quickly as it hit the road surface. We kept tucked in behind the timber waggon. At the top of The Rest over fifty vehicles were stranded. A police patrol man came into our bus.

'Did my man not warn you to stay at Arrochar?' he demanded.

'Aye, he did,' said one of the Scotsmen,' but we're no' stopping here; we're going on.'

'At your own risk,' said the sergeant.

'We'll be alright behind this waggon,' our driver tried to convince himself.

So cautiously we began the descent. Because of the formation of the mountains in that area the wind was being funnelled at great speed across the road that skirted Loch Restil, known as the Black Loch because of its great depth.

'It's a crack in the earth's surface,' I was informed.

Suddenly things began to happen. Visibility was so bad that we could only see the tail end of the timber lorry as it slid helplessly from the road to disappear completely into the engulfing black waters of the loch. Before we had time to comprehend what was happening our bus with a sickening lurch left the road to hit the water in a cascade of fury. Then with a tremendous jerk which threw us all from our seats the bus stopped.

The front of the bus was submerged. Water came in up to the third row of seats. We lay at a perilous angle. The old lady who had sat opposite to me lay in the water unconscious as her elderly husband panic stricken pleaded for help. The driver assisted by one of the Teddy Boys lifted

her clear and took her to a rear seat. The young woman with the ear muffs went to help and comfort her.

We then felt a sickening jolt from the rear of the bus. A smaller fourteen-seater bus had attempted to get through and had rammed us, successfully blocking our rear emergency exit door. We were trapped.

'Everyone sit still; try not to move as we do not know what is holding us from plunging into the loch. Keep as still as you can,' advised our driver.

The old men huddled at the back grumbling and muttering. The despised Teddy Boys were magnificent. They kept up our morale by singing and joking and assuring us. I gave them full marks.

We sat there for five, cold and frightening hours! Eventually the small bus was towed away from our stern and a police inspector entered from the rear.

'Everybody remain still and do not move until I give you individual permission. When you get out of the bus crawl on your hands and knees across the road to the small bus. If you attempt to stand you could easily be swept into the water. Now sir, you first.' He indicated me.

'I'll wait,' I said.

'Please do as I say; I'm trying to lighten the bus from the front.'

Cautiously I moved up the aisle while everyone held their breath. Out of the vehicle I flung myself to the snow covered ground and crawled across to the mini bus. I did not detect even a tiny breath of wind.

We all safely boarded the smaller bus and with a policeman acting as a paramedic with the old lady we set off for Inveraray. The little bus far exceeded her legal passenger capacity and again the Teddy Boys were magnificent.

At Inveraray the Argyll Arms had been prepared for us, but having thankfully partaken of a bowl of Scotch broth I went the few hundred yards to my friend's home.

The next morning I lay in bed until midday and until the police sergeant, who I know well, came to see me.

'The good Lord looks after his own; He was on your side last night!' said the policeman, 'do you know what saved you?'

'I've no idea,' I confessed, 'but those Teddy Boys deserve

a medal.'

'I've heard all about them. They are on their way to Lochgilphead now in our police car. It was a miracle. The cross member of the bus chassis hit a submerged pile and you were saved by a mere two inches. If that pile had been two inches shorter you would have all been in Kingdom Come by now.'

'What about the lorry driver and his mate?' I asked.

'We're dragging for them now,' was the response.

They never found them!

A Fyne Walk

I opened my eyes. The sunlight was already streaming into my bedroom and the skirl of bagpipes screaming into my ears. Murdo's ancient gramophone, a relic of the last century, wasn't doing justice to Harry Lauder.

I pulled aside the curtains. Loch Fyne was wearing a million dancing diamonds threaded on the chain of the wake of Hope's ferry boat as he plied the oars towards St Catherines. Dressed, I went to the breakfast room. Murdo was again winding up his treasure. As we ate our porridge the tempo of our spoons was conditioned to the speed of the turntable of the gramophone. For a few early moments our spoons beat a hearty reel to and fro our mouths but as the spring exhausted itself so the passage to our mouths became less lusty until Murdo would get up and give the winding handle a dose of his energy and our eating rhythm was restored.

Murdo scorned the 'troosers' and wore only the kilt. Did he wear anything under that kilt? It's still a mystery for if I ken I'm not giving anything away; like an Aberdonian!

The porridge pan was scraped and the result given to the expectant hens.

'Care for a walk along the lochside, Jack?' asked my host.

'Aye, certainly. It will help my porridge to come to terms with your home cured ham and the sausages,' I replied.

'Ye ken the Duke's deed?' asked Murdo.

'I was sorry to learn of his death, Murdo, for he and I became firm friends during the war. He was an amazing character.'

'Och, here comes two-ton Tessie!' exclaimed Murdo as we reached the bottom of the decline which led us to the water's edge.

Two-ton Tessie was a mere six and a half stones, almost five feet in height and so thin that if she had not been wearing stout walking shoes I'm sure the morning breeze would have blown her in the loch.

'Good morning te ye,' greeted Murdo, 'Ha'e ye met my friend Jack; Jack Richardson. He was here during the war?'

'Oh, aa ken aal aboot him, Murdo. He's a legend up here. Was it ye who was tangled up wi' Princess Marina?'

'Yes,' I replied in good Sassenach vocabulary.

'And there's a story aboot ye being on a buoy takkin' measurements.'

Just then a giant of a man carrying a wee bairn came round the bend and joined us.

'Jack, this is Roddy; Tessie's husband.'

He was at least six feet tall and built like a highland fortress. When he spoke the wildlife on the other side of the loch took off!

'Ye luk te be in good health, sir,' he said looking at me from stem to stern, 'I'm the undertaker frae Lochgilphead.'

'I'm involved in that kind of work myself,' I admitted, 'I'm a minister.'

'Noo aa ken ye; ye wor the minister who came to Mrs Paterson's when she wasna' deed,' Roddie said.

I now remembered him.

'You were the undertaker who came to the house to arrange the funeral and then went into the room to measure the body and the "dead" woman winked her eye at you,' I remembered.

'Aa got a real fright. She wasna' deed although the doctor had pronoonced her deed. I had a wasted journey. It was a bad week for me. I was requested by the Glasgow Social Services to arrange a funeral for a wee widow woman. Aa went te her hoose, knocked on the door and the corpse opened it!'

'What; a walking corpse, or had you had a wee dram too many?'

'No, the wee body was still alive and kicking. She looked kind o' funny at me when I said the first thing that came into my mind, "I've just called to see hoo ye are keeping, Mrs Paterson." As soon as I got hame I rang up the Social Services to complain and to seek my expenses but they claimed that they knew that she was still alive but wanted me to have all the funeral arrangements ready, "just in case" as they would be responsible for her funeral. It's a cruel worrld at times!'

Murdo saw Roddie looking in a concentrated manner at him so decided to carry on with our perambulations.

'That man gie's me the creeps. I expected him to get his tape measure out to size me up!'

We walked slowly taking in all the sights and scenes of wonderful nature. A solitary swan scarcely disturbed the smooth surface of the loch as it gracefully glided.

'Sad about that swan,' said Murdo, 'It's a cob and it lost its pen last year and has wandered up and down this loch grieving.'

'What happened?' I asked.

'In defending its cygnets against the attack of a fox it lost its life; but look, there's a rabbit!'

'Oh, let me get hold of Roger; he'll be after it like a shot,' I cried.

'No, leave it to me. Come here, Roger,' he commanded the dog.

Roger came. Murdo knelt down and slowly stroked the dog then whispered to him, 'See that rabbit? I want you to go slowly up to it and not to scare it.'

Turning his attention to the furry little bunny he spoke

again. 'Dinna be afraid; the dog won't hurt you. Just stay put and dinna run awa.'

Strangely it all occurred as he planned it. Roger walked up to the stationary rabbit, sniffed at it and then turned to look at Murdo.

'All right; off you go now, gently,' he bade the rabbit which hopped away without being followed by Roger.

By this time we were in sight of Charlie's widow's cottage. Smoke curled lazily from the chimney, doing a disappearing act among the surrounding trees.

Charlie had been the local butcher. I had known him well but had not seen Flora his wife, since his sudden and untimely death. She made us welcome and put the kettle on.

'It's a little too early for a dram,' was her excuse but her coffee was well percolated. We talked of Charlie.

'He had a good funeral. We put him away in grand style.

All the Lodge members were there. The organist played his favourite tune as they carried him into the kirk; 'Sheep may safely graze'.

'Aye,' said Murdo, 'I suppose that they can noo that he's no longer aboot, but the deer were aye always safe from him!'

'What do you mean?' I asked.

'Flora kens aboot this. Charlie and his cousin Sandy went oot one night poaching venison. After a couple of hours they found a young stag hiding behind a bush. They were creeping silently up upon the timorous creature, taking care to scarcely breath when Charlie suddenly broke wind...and the deer broke cover. No venison in his shop that week!'

'Can ye mind when he stumbled across a couple o' lasses sunbathing in the nude doon by the loch, Flora? He decided to share his find wi' Sandy and they went alang te find that one o' them was Sandy's own daughter! She was a Sunday School teacher!'

I thought that it was time for us to continue our walk before things became too revealing.

Nearer to the town we arrived at Fiona's 'Single-end'. This was an apartment at the end of a block of flats intended for a single person. Fiona was one of the nicest ladies I have ever met. Always courteous and extremely generous and with a sparkling sense of humour she was almost eighty years old. She made us welcome and we refused further sustenance but remained to chat.

'Fiona, would you mind if I asked you why you never married?' I asked.

'Not at all. Murdo knows anyway! During the first war the East Sussex Regiment was stationed here for training. I fell in love with a young officer. He was everything that a young lass dreamed about. Father liked him and soon he was a regular guest at our table. He asked me to marry him and I accepted.'

'I know what's coming; he was killed in France!' I ventured.

'Not so,' said Fiona. 'After the war was over I heard nothing from him so I wrote to his home address. His wife answered my letter!'

On our way back to Murdo's home we had to pass Duncan's peculiar 'but and ben'. Peculiar it was for it was a square building with all sides equal reaching up to a chimney that was taller than the house itself. We went into the only room. The walls were covered with portraits of Duncan dressed in army uniform and masonic regalia.

'That's either a picture of the Pope or of you in masonic rig,' I teased, 'What lodge are you in?'

'Lodge number four, Inveraray,' was the proud reply, 'but it's now numbered sixty-four which it shouldn't be.'

He went at great length to explain why the number had been changed so I wished to change the subject.

'I see that you were a sergeant in the army, Duncan.'

'Aye, but not when I left the army!'

'Ah, you gained a commission?'

'I was recommended but finished up as a corporal!'

'Why?'

'After the allied landings in Normandy we had pushed up into Belgium. We had taken the brunt of the advance. Our numbers were depleted and we needed to re-form and be rested.'

'Yes; I can understand that,' I remarked.

'So we were sent well back behind the fighting to a rehabilitation camp. On this particular day the duty officer was a man who had never been near to any fighting. I think that he was R.A.S.C. Catering. He was a dandy if ever there was one. The meal was rotten! It lay like a thick slime on the plates. Remarks were made that it was a mixture of French snails and tadpoles. No one could stomach eating such rubbish.

'In came the duty officer.

' "Any complaints?" he demanded in a haughty tone.

' "Yes sir," I spoke up, "this food is not fit to be served up to us. This is the sergeants' mess and even we would not offer this offal to the privates."

'The officer looked at my plate which I offered to him but which he didn't take.

' "Nothing wrong with it, sergeant; you Jocks are much too fussy. Just wait until you get back into civvy street you'll eat worse than this. You'll be back to your oats!"

' "But sir, smell it," I requested.

'I went to him with it. He refused to smell it.

' "Then ye'll taste it," I said and rammed the plateful into his pale cream features. What an exhilarating moment it was. I felt good. Everyone cheered; but I didn't feel too good the next day when I was before the colonel. I asked for a sample of the meal to be produced for my defence but I reckon the cook had destroyed the evidence. I became a corporal!'

'So did Hitler!' I said as Duncan almost kicked me out.

Maire, Murdo's wife, asked me if I would take her to the pierhead to see the Duke's funeral the next day.

We stood well back as we watched the coffin being loaded on to the galleon which then sailed down the loch towards Dunoon. A huge standard depicting a galleon flew from the mast. As the dirge of the pipers filtered through the glens so a tear filtered down my cheeks. Maire sobbed openly...oh, my...she was married to a McDonald!

We watched the army contingents depart together with the captains and the crowd. Corporal Duncan was there in his kilt. Some other villain was there too; with his can. For as we reached my car I saw that the petrol cap was missing. My tank had been syphoned. Ah, well, as Murdo would have said, I was in Campbell country!!

The purpose of my visit to that area was not merely to walk alongside the loch, no matter how pleasing that may be or to watch funerals of bygone friends but to preach in the kirk upon the Sabbath day!

Dougal was the minister. He was ready for a dram at any time of the day or night preferably partaken up in Glen Shira. In the congregation were Murdo and his brother Peter from the Isle of Skye; an elder of the kirk there and at one time Provost of Portree. Two other brothers were in the choir, Hope and Dodo. Kirsty adorned the front pew and preferred the gaelic wording of the paraphrased psalms.

'My text is from psalm 137; "How can I sing the Lord's song in a strange land?" '

Murdo and Peter stowed their bonnets into their sporrans among the bawbees set aside for the collection and settled down for the sermon.

'Och,' I heard an elderly elder remark, 'he's wearing the rags of popery!' My surplice almost became a badge of shame and heresy! After the service was over we adjourned to Kirsty's Temperance hotel for lunch and Murdo and Peter to be revived with a non-temperance beverage.

'What did you make o' Jack's sermon?' Kirsty asked the others.

Peter answered, 'No' much!'

'Why do you say that?' I objected. 'What was wrong with it?'

'Wrang? Far better ask what was right wi' it. I fell to be thinking aboot Noah and his ark,' said Peter.

'But I wasn't preaching about Noah and his ark!'

'I ken that, too.'

Kirsty sought to pour oil on Noah's troubled flood water and said, 'Peter, I looked at you in the kirk. It wasn't Noah ye were thinking about. Ye were aye scanning the ladies in the pews.'

'Just at their bonnets,' protested Peter.

'Because their legs were hidden from you!' Kirsty insisted.

Peter tried to turn the conversation to the weather but Murdo took over.

'I liked the sermon because Jack kept to scripture.'

'Ye didna show much appreciation for you passed the plate to me!'

Prison and Pub

'So they've caught up with you finally and about time too, you wiley old rascal!' said my friend, or rather acquaintance, Andy. 'When do you go in?'

'Next week,' I admitted.

'Cor, I wouldn't relish a spell in prison no matter how short the term, I wonder what it's like when the big doors clang behind you!' said my teenage grand-daughter, Naomi, 'Will we be able to visit you?'

'Hold hard, me hearties,' I said. 'I'm only going in for five hours.'

Andy was interested; 'Is it some kind of corrective exercise or something to do with community work as a punishment?'

'I had better come clean. Yes, I'm going into prison but only to give a lecture.'

'To the warders, no doubt.'

'No; to the Lifers' summer school!'

'You're kidding, aren't you? there may be killers and arsonists in that lot. Aren't you afraid?'

'Not in the least. I lectured there last year and thoroughly enjoyed it.'

'Hey, grandad, you might be held hostage,' said Naomi hopefully.

'I wouldn't mind; the conditions there are really better than some of the homes I have been in.'

'What was it like when you went there last year?' Naomi was interested!

'I drove up to the car park. Another car came in alongside me and a very tough crew got out of it. I didn't know where the entrance was so I asked these people. They obligingly offered to show me.

' "Are you visiting someone?" [I'm really naive!]

' "Yes; my brother. We've come from Chesterfield but we come regularly."

Putting both feet into it I plunged, "How long is he in for?"

' "Life!, he killed his wife's lover!"

'I had to pass through a complicated security system before I was finally encased behind electrified fences and steel doors with a minder that resembled King Kong and who carried so many keys that he was almost bow-legged.'

'Did you see any prisoners?' asked Naomi.

'Dozens! In my class there were twelve lifers including murderers! But they were so nice, mainly young, that if I had not known their history I would have gladly welcomed

them to my own home.'

Naomi seemed to be on edge to tell me something.

'We had great excitement last night, grandad. The police helicopter was over our home for over an hour. There was an escaped convict from your prison lurking about some-where and maybe in our outhouses. The helicopter's powerful searchlight shone right into my bedroom. Then the police arrived with dogs.'

'Did they catch him?' I asked.

'I don't know but I hope not.'

'Why on earth not?' exploded Andy.

'Well, all those dogs and police and helicopters after him; it didn't seem fair!'

I'm hoping that I can manage to escape next week so I can continue writing this book in freedom!

Besides prisons there are other 'Ps' involved in parish life. The village pump, the village parson and, of course the pub. Like all things and as the hymn so truly says, 'Change and decay in all around I see', even these seemingly traditionalised and well established pillars of village life have changed dramatically.

The pump has gone. The focal point for the village gossips who went there for their water and returned with the juice of scandal has disappeared to be occasionally substituted in times of drought by the 'stand pipes'.

'The parson's freehold' is no longer concentrated on a single parish. Many have four or even five parishes to care for so the old time house-visiting vicar finds it impossible to recreate that intimate relationship he had with his parishioners.

What of the pub? Its roots go back to biblical days. The best known are the inn where there was no room and the wayside inn that gave sustenance to the traveller brought in by the Good Samaritan. If there is any change there it is for the good. Many such establishments now cater, as they should do, for families and provide food as well as drink.

Our village pub had been offering hospitality for over four hundred years. Its mellow bricks were as warm as the welcome inside. Here there were cosy little snugs and intimate nooks. Here for centuries farmers had met after mart and put the world to rights. Here lovers had met and housewives relaxed. The whole atmosphere was not one of stale beer and sawdust but of home and comfort.

So it was with fear and trepidation that I learnt that the

brewery was planning to demolish it and build a modern hotel.

'I have called this meeting to seek your views on the planned alterations to our pub,' I explained to the many parishioners who were gathered, quite rightly within the pub itself. To encourage their thoughts Albert and Jean, mine hosts, had supplied the first drinks without charge. The outcome of the meeting was that we had to oppose any demolition of our village landmark.

'We do not appreciate your term of "chromium-plated gin palace" applied to our proposed improvements to the inn in your village.'

So ran the gist of an angry communication I received from the brewery. I replied at length with courtesy but firmness. The outcome was a compromise. The exterior would remain as it was but the inside would be 'modernised'. The little snugs would disappear and the brewery very kindly sent me drawings of their proposed interior decorations. The result was excellent. The brewery bosses seeking to win the favour and approval of St Peter or perhaps Bacchus offered the first day's takings upon re-opening to the church and allowed us to have a coffee morning on the premises on the very first morning.

'You're behind the bar, Ethel, together with the Mothers' Union, not pulling pints but serving coffee.'

'Any chance of a sly pint?' asked Elsie from Church View and a future churchwarden.

'No; and not even Gaelic coffee!'

Things went splendidly. The farmers turned up in force. The till rang merrily as the church bells rang a summons to all within the parish bounds. They summoned others; outsiders; the press!

'Let's have you on the doorstep of the pub with a farmer to be photographed,' said the *Express* reporter. They found the fattest and most prosperous looking of the farmers and he and I sat on the doorstep outside the pub in brilliant sunshine drinking coffee. This let all Hell loose!

After the publication of that photograph in the national

press I received obscene and threatening phone calls and a mountain of abusive letters.

'I never thought that I would see the Devil himself dressed as a clergyman!' ran one letter.

'Encouraging young people along the road to damnation,' read another.

'The demon drink has won another victory against all decency.'

'Resign!' was the brief suggestion in one letter from a Welsh cleric!

'You've gone to Hell; don't drag others down with you.' and all because I imbibed coffee with a very sober and God-fearing farmer!

Did the brewery give me a bottle of hooch as a reward for all this pub-licity? No, but they gave to our church two hundred pounds. I was criticised for accepting it.

It fair drives one to drink!

Pilgrim Father

The Mission to Seamen in New York gave me a splendid welcome. Their organist blasted forth one of my favourite pieces of music specially for me and then gave me two copies of music and words. It is Sibelius' 'Finlandia'. The choir from its appearance was drawn from the nearby United Nations Building and had combined with the Gospel Singers. It was tuneful and colourful. After I had given them the Word, in English, I expected cookies and coke but even in the New World they stick to the ubiquitous currant scones and tea.

'Let's see what we have in here,' said the bearded, coloured customs officer at Kennedy Airport. He opened my case exposing all my unmentionables. He picked up my razor.

'What are you going to do with this?'

'A good man needs to shave!'

He stroked his own beard which hid a smile. 'You a minister and tell us, man, about people like the prophets. Did you ever see a cleanshaven prophet?'

'I've never seen a prophet,' I confessed.

'You will; there're lots of them in New York!'

Then confidentially he whispered through his curly, black fungus 'Did you know that there are as many different religions in Manhattan as there are days in the year?'

'Oh, come off it,' I ventured, 'Surely you mean as many weeks, not days.'

'No man, I mean days. You'll find out.'

'And what are you?' I was bold to ask.

'Me? I'm my own religion, man. What are you?' he replied.

'I'm C. of E.'

'Spell it out, man, spell it out. You're not a communist?'

He replaced my razor, picked up my Bible and said, 'Hum.'

My hostess had provided a sleek, imposing looking Cadillac to convey us from the airport to the hotel on Manhattan Island. As we neared 54th Avenue crowds of excited teenagers surged towards the car clamouring for a glimpse of the occupants. They cheered and shouted.

'A great welcome, this,' I said to Ethel, 'I didn't know that we were so well-known!'

The excited crowd extended all the way to the hotel but before we reached it the driver informed us that the crowds of fanatical teenagers were not waiting to welcome me, but the Beatles who were to stay in the hotel opposite the one we were to stay in and that they were to be driven there in a similar black Cadillac! I had tasted five minutes of fame anyway! These youngsters were so determined to see the Beatles that one girl of seventeen actually climbed up the exterior of that hotel for twenty floors in order to get an autograph. I would have given her mine without all that fuss.

After ten days at the World Fair on Long Island we journeyed to Cooperstown, the birthplace of Fenimore Cooper who wrote *The Last of the Mohicans*. Here is a wonderland; here is a Paradise of beauty and here is where our gracious hostess lived. Alan was our chauffeur.

'Did you know that there are as many religions in New York as there are days in the year?' I asked.

'Oh, undoubtedly; anyone can set up a new religion in this country. There's a certain gullibility about Americans. I'll take you to see the Cardiff Giant just to prove my point.'

There is a complete village, preserved and maintained as it was in the days of the early settlers there. Alan took us in that village to where the Cardiff Giant lay in stoney silence and ignominious incognition.

'Over a hundred years ago,' began Alan, 'this fossilized giant was exhumed by an archaeologist. It was confirmed by the most emminent of scientists and experts that this was indeed the prehistoric remains of a time when, to quote the Bible, Jack, "giants lived on earth." '

'He's a whopper,' I remarked.

'You are gullible too,' laughed Alan. 'For almost fifty years this was a prized exhibit. There was no other like it in the world. Then the discoverer was on the point of discovering even greater antiquities in the world-to-come. As he was dying he revealed how he had constructed the "giant" and how he had "aged" it. It had been a most successful hoax!'

Niagara was no hoax. They really do, at times, turn off the falls! From the black squirrels of Niagara we went to Quebec and on a cruise up the Saguenay beyond Taddousac, the old Red Indian kingdom. Again tradition spoke of giants but this time of one-legged giants which used to roam there among the one eyed pygmies of North America! How did the one-legged giants walk? We held a midnight service somewhere up the coast of that remote area.

It was when we reached Quebec again that we needed prayers! The Chateau Frontenach was to be our hotel but when we got there chaos ruled in the foyer. People were shouting and threatening. I pushed through the multitude which milled about the reception desk and caught the eye of the receptionist.

'The Reverend Richardson,' I introduced myself.

'One moment, sir.'

He fished in a pigeon hole and found my reservation.

'You are room 624 but you cannot get the keys.'

'Why not?'

'There's a strike and everyone is being put out of the hotel. I dare not give you the keys!'

'But where am I to go?'

'Don't know sir; can't help you!

Ethel and I were thousands of miles from home, in a foreign country with nowhere to lay our heads.

'I'm going to see the manager,' I instructed Ethel, 'he'll have to find us alternative accommodation.'

It was my turn to be gullible!

'You can't see the manager; he's seeing no one,' said the Gestapo working as a secretary, bodyguard and bouncer. With her grey hair she looked like Mount Fuji!

I gave her a withering glance; it didn't work. I tried to get past her but the detour was too great. She had feet like frying pans and one of them barred my path like a soggy omelette. I turned to leave and she sat down. I then made a mad rush for the manager's door and succeeded. She came after me like a landslide!

'Sorry sir, I thought that he was leaving,' she apologised to her lord and master. He was a wimp!

In French he told me to leave. I bamboozled him by replying in broad Geordie. He must have thought that I was a Hungarian!

'Get out of my office,' he ordered in English.

'Not until I get the key to my room which is paid for in advance!'

I sat down. 'I'm staying here until I get it and if I do not get it soon I'll be in touch with the consul.' I didn't know if there was a consul there and evidently he didn't either.

'I dare not give you the key but seeing as you are a priest I will give you an address. You will be able to have free accommodation but may have to pay for services,' he offered.

'Fair enough: I appreciate your difficulties,' I replied as I waited for him to scribble an address for me.

I made my way through the thronging dissidents in the foyer and espied Ethel talking to an elderly couple.

'This is Mr and Mrs Clinton. Mr Clinton is secretary to a union.'

'What a carry on,' I remarked, 'I've been in to the manager and got an address to which we can go for the night,' I exclaimed triumphantly.

'So have I', said Mr Clinton, 'I was able to see the manager because of my union affiliation. Here's the address I have been given.'

'Oh, it's the same as mine. Let's share a taxi,' I suggested.

There were literally hundreds queueing for taxis. As the evening wore on we began to get anxious. Then a taxi accommodated us.

'Where to?' asked the taxi driver.

I presented him with my slip of paper. He perused and laughed. I was wearing my clerical collar.

'Do you really want to go to this address?'

'Well,' I said, 'We must have somewhere to sleep tonight.'

'You'll not get much sleep there at anytime; it's a brothel!'

Eventually we found a room at an unfinished motel bordering a cemetery. It had no electricity or water but had a massive mural of a naked woman above the beds. She faced the graveyard! So our pilgrimage was over. I'll go by Mayflower next time!

Epilogue

Filled with vision, fired by at least a spirit of service and eager to get the bit between my teeth I was ordained in Durham Cathedral. It was an unusual ceremony in that I was ordained while standing and not in the normal posture of kneeling. It follows that such things happen to me but in this case it was courteous and well meant.

'David'; that was the other ordinand for only two of us were to be ordained that day; 'cannot kneel because of his war wound,' said the Bishop. 'As we all know his leg is permanently stiff and I think it would be rather odd to the congregation to see one ordained kneeling while the other stands.'

I found inspiration in Isaiah Chapter 6, verse 8: 'Here am I; send me.' Presumptuously I stood in the old prophet's shoes. Now, looking back over a period in excess of forty years, I wonder if I have served well. I know my many shortcomings but without holding an inquest, perhaps it is good to look back on some varied moments of my ministry. Maybe Isaiah would not approve of all that I have done or endeavoured to do, but in my weakness I have tried.

I have served in a town parish where I met up with young mothers and mature tigers; wiley parishioners and tame foxes, sea cadets and the Girls' Friendly Society.

Then I moved in exalted circles as chaplain to an earl inheriting a tradition that involved a giant worm, 'that sucked aal the coos dry and ate up little bairns. It had a greet big mooth and goggly eyes.' Such was the Lambton worm! The spiritual tenants of the upper rooms never worried me as much as the turbulent residents of the parish.

The call of the sea was insistent. Like a mistress it never gives up and I found myself awaiting appointment in Portsmouth barracks. From the Red Sea to the Arctic circle we showed the flag, and I preached the Word in Scotland in a tin hut; in Genoa sharing the service with a clergyman called Andrew McVicar who wore no shirt! Tarhuna on the edge of the Sahara saw me preaching at an oasis where the week before glamorous film stars had cavorted while making a film. After amoebic dysentery, injuries sustained in an overturned vehicle which was being driven by a Lebanese and a spell in hospital with a War Graves Commission representative and an atheist army captain. I was holding forth in Malta when we had a bomb alert. Lisbon was interesting for I preached to several nationals at once. They thought that I spoke pidgin English! Port Steward in Northern Ireland was peaceful and safe in those days but we did manage, with evil intent, to get the presbyterian abstainer who was mayor, drunk in the wardroom after matins. I landed at Culdrose from a helicopter to preach to naval air personnel again in a Nissen hut.

Eventually I returned to parish work and had such a happy time at Bishopton. Here we had 'live and dead' sales, refurnished the church and demolished the poltergeist which disturbed the soccer results coming through on the television. I preached at a harvest service at Lindisfarne, Holy Island where the church was festooned with fishing nets and lobster pots and a whacking great lobster hung from the pulpit. It is the custom there to give the lobster to the preacher. In contrast I preached at a similar service on Teesside where the church looked like a grocer's store with tins of provisions stacked up on the altar.

Then another move to where there were molehills, antique sales and Morris dancers and leaking roofs and wet-rot decks.

I have suffered the hazards of my calling in the gastronomic field; organic and non-organic. Among the organic was home made port wine which sealed my lips like super glue and swilled around my stomach for three days like cement that refused to set. Worse than that was the product of the sea presented to me in a soup dish in Toulon; *bouillabaisse* which smelt like and tasted like another brand of adhesive! I have eaten swordfish in the Mediterranean, rainbow trout on Long Island flown from the Rocky Mountains, and octopus in Palestine. The most repugnant was cush-cush partaken with the Bedouins where I was terrified lest I was chosen to receive the tit-bit; the sheep's eye! In Inveraray I had the double joy of haggis and clootie dumpling; both sumptuous and to be recommended. My favourite is still leek pudding, with Oxo and on a winter's day! I steadfastly refused birds' nest soup and never fancied those slimey things that crawl about my garden; snails. Still, every man to his own fancy.

I have met vicars who rejected the miraculous, those who dispensed with any prayer book in order to present 'trendy' services. Their gimmicks never had any lasting results and were more often negative. There were others, by the grace of God, who were hard working, sincere servants burning themselves out for the sake of others. Such men have always been an inspiration.

So now I come to the stage when I must ask myself, 'Have I fulfilled a good and fruitful ministry?'

I wasn't ordained merely to travel the world or to eat exotic meals. I have always endeavoured to spread the Word and to do so with dignity yet humour for God gave us all the capacity to enjoy life and work. I can see the joy and the humour of Christ in the gospels. God gave us the ability to laugh in a way that no other creature can.

So I have tried in this and my other books to get a serious message over and yet to raise a laugh. I do sincerely hope that you too have enjoyed this as much as I enjoyed writing it.